WHAT OTHERS ARE
WHEN JUSTICE IS

In a world where so many people are excluded and marginalized, the issues of justice and equity seem to be an alien concept or at best a convenient political sound bite reserved for election campaigns. This book offers a refreshing, challenging and alternative perspective on social justice. Jesus speaks into the madness of this 21st century with a clarity and relevance that will change the world if only we will listen to him.

—*General André Cox, International Leader of The Salvation Army*

Throughout this book—amplified by questions for reflection, prayers and case studies—the authors remind us of the intricate relationship between imago Dei, humanity and justice. This is a must-read for individuals who want to engage and respond to the call of divine justice through a global lens, in an honest, relevant and impactful way.

—*Dr. Ndunge Kiiti, Professor of International Development and Director, Center for Faith, Justice and Global Engagement, Houghton College, New York*

The psalmist reminds us that righteousness and justice are the foundation of God's throne (see Psalm 97:2). If justice is foundational to the creator of all things then it is foundational for all aspects of our lives, too. In giving close attention to this book, we are encouraged to do just that—to deeply consider how the foundation of justice may be demonstrated in our lives.

—*Colonel Janet Munn, Training Principal, The Salvation Army Officer Training College, Australia Eastern Territory*

This book, along with the heart and mission of its authors, offers us not only the why but the how to wade through complex justice issues with a firm and simple resolve to live like Jesus, right here and now. We live in a world with a black and desperate backdrop of injustice. We are easily paralyzed from action by fear, confusion and a lack of strategy. But we need not be. This book offers scriptural and modern resources to wake us from our slumber, break off our fear and help us act justly. Justice is the expression of God's kingdom coming—it's what Jesus lived and taught us to pray. Everyone should not only read this book but put it into practice. Be warned—it could change your life!

—*Major Danielle Strickland, Corps Officer, Edmonton Crossroads Community Church*

When Justice is the Measure provides clear and compelling biblical insights that reflect God's heart for all people. As a Christ-follower, if you want to help build a more just and peaceful world, this is a powerful and life-changing resource.

—*Dr. Geoff Tunnicliffe, Chief Executive Officer/Secretary General, World Evangelical Alliance*

WHEN JUSTICE IS THE MEASURE

M. Christine MacMillan

Don Posterski

James E. Read

Foreword
GEANETTE SEYMOUR

Published by The Salvation Army, Canada and Bermuda Territory
2 Overlea Blvd., Toronto, Ontario M4H 1P4
Phone: 416-425-2111; fax: 416-422-6120
www.salvationarmy.ca

Cover Design: Timothy Cheng
Cover Art: Fritz Eichenberg, *Christ of the Breadlines* (1953) © Estate of Fritz
Eichenberg/SODRAC, Montreal/VAGA, New York (2013)
Layout and Design: Timothy Cheng

Printed in Canada
ISBN: 978-0-88857-512-8

The assistance of these contributors in preparing this book is greatly
appreciated:

Members of the Territorial Literature Council, staff of the Editorial
Department (Editor-in-Chief and Literary Secretary: Geoff Moulton; Copy
Editor: Pamela Richardson)

TABLE OF CONTENTS

FOREWORD

W*hen Justice is the Measure* is a book written from the hearts and minds of three people to impact the heart and mind of the reader.

When justice is the measure—

People everywhere have opportunities to flourish ...

People everywhere are able to access

> Education
> Employment
> Shelter and food
> Government and social services.

People everywhere are able to develop their God-given capacities

> Intellectual
> Moral and
> Spiritual.

People everywhere are able to live in

> Functional families
> Supportive communities and
> Social order that protects human rights.

When justice is the measure—

> The young and those who are older,
> Those living in less-developed countries and those
> Living in more-developed countries,
> All have opportunities to learn and work,
> To live with measures of dignity
> And pursue their personal potential.

The authors—who were all part of The Salvation Army's International Social Justice Commission when they wrote this book—know that when justice is the measure, people who know justice will be unwilling to accept less for others than they have for themselves. Those who live justly will work so that others will be able to receive justice, and injustice issues will be challenged and overcome.

When justice is the measure, men and women, who know themselves to be the children of God, will live a life that shows the marks of justice and work for justice for others.

This book shows what justice looks like, what it aims to achieve and challenges us to measure ourselves and our lifestyle against that benchmark. As you read, may God grant you insight into his vision.

Colonel Geanette Seymour, Director, The Salvation Army
International Social Justice Commission

ACKNOWLEDGMENTS

The authors want to express their thanks to the people whose stories have made the writing of this book possible. We are especially indebted to Vânia Batista, Paul du Plessis, Campbell Roberts and Carol Seiler. Other anonymous contributors will never know we have told their stories, but that does not diminish our gratitude.

The Scripture quotations contained herein are from the *New Revised Standard Version Bible*, copyright, 1989, by the Division of Christian Education of the National Council of the Churches of Christ in the U.S.A. Used by permission. All rights reserved.

INTRODUCTION

This book interprets the Bible, and the life and ministry of Jesus in particular, with justice as the measure.

Jesus' first days were marked with poverty. His family was on the road and there was no room available—anywhere. A smelly animal stall was his starting place in life. The details surrounding the night of his birth are largely unknown. Perhaps there was a midwife staying in a nearby hotel. Surely someone came with water and a basin to bathe the newborn child. Whatever the specifics were, we are left to guess. What we do know is the beginning was bleak. Only the bare essentials were there.

We also know that the birth did not go unnoticed. The shepherds who were on duty out in the night air were honoured with the first birth announcement. They rushed to be the early worshippers of this special child. The shepherds didn't think much about the place where Jesus was born. They had been in many animal pens before. They were comfortable kneeling on the straw. They didn't appreciate the incongruity of the Son of God's meagre beginning.

The quandary for those of us who follow Christ is to link the first days of Jesus with his continuing mission. The honoured shepherds were poor. The rewards of their work barely put food on their tables, yet, they were the first worshippers. As examples of God's bias toward the poor, the shepherds are historical spiritual heroes. They remind us that God's heart still leans toward those who are pressed to live with less.

Early in his adult ministry, Jesus returned home to Nazareth. Rumours were spreading about his teaching and miraculous powers, and he was invited to speak at the local synagogue where he had worshipped as a child. His audience that morning was filled with skeptics. "What is Mary and Joseph's son doing now? Who does he think he is?"

Sensing a special moment, Jesus took the occasion to lay out his mission. He read from the revered prophet Isaiah: "The Spirit of the

Lord is upon me, because he has anointed me to bring good news to the poor. He has sent me to proclaim release to the captives and recovery of sight to the blind, to let the oppressed go free, to proclaim the year of the Lord's favour" (Luke 4:18-19). And when he finished, Jesus rolled up the scroll and essentially said, "Let me tell you what this means."

The essence of Jesus' mission is captured in a single vision—one vision with two dimensions. Jesus' hope for a restored humanity has a double focus: people who are *spiritually poor* and people who are *socially poor.*

SPIRITUALLY POOR: Jesus begins with a personal claim: "The Spirit of the Lord is upon me." I have been touched by God and I am in touch with God. And the good news I bring to those of you who are spiritually poor is, you can be in touch with God, too.

SOCIALLY POOR: Jesus understands the systemic nature of social poverty. He sees people in poverty as those who are held captive. They are oppressed and victims of their circumstances. People living in social poverty need eyes to see beyond the barriers that imprison them and to be freed to explore a new future.

The chapters that follow will reveal over and over again that Jesus lived right—that righteousness was his way of life. The material will also show that Jesus repeatedly righted wrongs—that pursuing justice for the sake of others was his intent and practice. The mission of Jesus had two cutting edges. He awakened in the morning with a vision for people's spiritual well-being and he envisioned opportunities for people whose plight in life was curtailed by oppressive constraints and life-denying forces. Jesus lived right and righted wrongs. And for those of us who claim to be followers of Jesus, his mission on earth in his time is our mission on earth in our time.

The book is divided into four major sections, each focusing on a major principle of biblical social justice. Readers are invited to examine the Gospel accounts with the measure of justice in mind. They are encouraged to share their thinking with others and prayerfully discern the needs of our world. The lens is then turned on Salvation Army ministry. The parts of the book that tell Salvation Army stories draw on historical and current examples of justice-motivated ministry. They relate first-person accounts of Christine MacMillan, with reflections from her decades of ministry service. But the principles are not for just one denomination or one time frame. They issue a call across the full range of expressions of Christian ministry and urge readers everywhere to strategically pursue ministry mandates in the future with Jesus' justice truly as the measure.

The four chapters can be read in the order in which they are presented or they can be read in a sequence that suits the reader better. Each justice principle stands on its own and also supplements the other principles. The book can be read by an individual or (as the authors had in mind) by a group. There is material to inform individuals and challenge them personally, but there is something extra to be gained by engaging the material as a group since social justice is a shared good and it invites community engagement. As the Bible says, "How very good and pleasant it is when kindred live together in unity!" (Psalm 133:1).

In The Salvation Army we proclaim that Jesus died to be the Saviour of the world. There is no debating that. We proclaim that Jesus is the divine Son of God through whom everyone can have eternal life. But have we underplayed the commitment of Jesus to *justice here and now*? We cannot encounter Jesus fully until we embrace him as an advocate for the poor and vulnerable. We are at risk of dwarfing the mission mandate of Jesus in our own time when we limit the attention we give to Jesus as a justice advocate for people who are poor, vulnerable and excluded.

The historical record will show that in the early days, William Booth boldly and passionately addressed injustices on the streets of London, England. It will show that other pioneer Salvationists tackled social injustice in parts of the world beyond London. Righting the wrongs of this world mattered to them just as seeking people's personal salvation did.

The justice motive for ministry may have become obscured in generations that followed the Founder, but it does not have to stay that way. When Jesus' justice is the measure and people or organizations fail, there is the privilege of beginning again.

We need to be painfully aware that God's creation is groaning. We need to lament the fact that so many people are scavenging just to survive. We need to know that children and women live daily with vulnerabilities over which they have no control. We need to hear the sounds of gunfire that shatter peace in lands near and far. We need to weep at the waste of human life perpetuated by family and government dysfunction. Even as we envision a world where justice is the measure, we know that injustice is often the reality. Still, we believe the people of God are mandated to be creative agents of mercy in the middle of the messes.

If you engage yourself with the issues that follow, you may also conclude that it is time to embrace a fresh vision that makes more space, prompts more prayer, allocates more resources and expends more energy in *seeking justice together.*

One last word of introduction. This book was written while the authors were part of The Salvation Army's International Social Justice Commission (ISJC). It is meant to make a contribution to the mission of the ISJC to raise strategic voices to advocate with the world's poor and oppressed. Our hope is that those who read this book will by motivated to connect more fully. Visit the website: www.salvationarmy.org/isjc.

M. Christine MacMillan, Don Posterski and James E. Read

CHAPTER 1

INCLUDING THE EXCLUDED

There is no longer Jew or Greek, there is no longer slave or free, there is no longer male and female; for all of you are one in Christ Jesus (Galatians 3:28).

A ll who place their faith in Christ are members of God's family. The categories that section us off from each other are stripped away. We are all included in the same family clan—equal in the sight of God.

No Jew or Greek—our ethnicities are blended in one humanity.

No slave or free—economics no longer determine personal worth.

No male and female—superiority of one over the other is subdued.

No racial superiority, no social segregation, no hierarchy. We all belong to a new society.

For all of us, our equality of identity is being "in Christ" as followers of our risen Lord.

No one is excluded from the family reunion.

Experiencing exclusion is traumatic. It is like being unfairly "red-carded" while playing soccer. You were on the playing field, passing the ball on offence and intercepting passes on defence. Then suddenly, a biased referee claimed you inflicted an intentional foul on the opposition, and you were on the sidelines and out of the game. Tragically, in real life, many people never leave the sidelines and get into the game. Without even breaking the rules or inflicting pain on anyone else, they are red-carded. They are ineligible to play in the game of life.

Showing Compassion Toward Social Outsiders

Our world can be an unkind place. Caste systems have many configurations. Social judgment parades with many faces. People who are disfigured, physically disabled or mentally handicapped, and even kids who are bullied on school playgrounds can be victims of injustice without being guilty of anything but being themselves. They are outsiders. They are simply excluded. And their unjust exclusion is humiliating.

Encountering God in the Biblical Story

Give yourself permission to travel into a new spiritual place. Take permission to rest in that new place before exploring your next journey.

- Read the three texts below consecutively and out loud.
- Without any discussion, read the passages in silence and let the text speak to you.
- Ponder your thoughts in silence.
- Share your thoughts with each other, without discussion.
- After everyone has shared, invite each person to make one concluding comment.

When Jesus had come down from the mountain, great crowds followed him; and there was a leper who came to him and knelt before him, saying, "Lord, if you choose, you can make me clean." He stretched out his hand and touched him, saying, "I do choose. Be made clean!" Immediately his leprosy was cleansed (Matthew 8:1-3).

On the way to Jerusalem Jesus was going through the region between Samaria and Galilee. As he entered a village, 10 lepers approached him. Keeping their distance, they called out, saying, "Jesus, Master, have mercy on us!" When he saw them, he said to them, "Go and show yourselves to the priests." And as they went, they were made clean. Then one of them, when he saw that he was healed, turned back, praising God with a loud voice. He prostrated himself at Jesus' feet and thanked him. And he was a Samaritan. Then Jesus asked, "Were not 10 made clean? But the other nine, where are they? Was none of them found to return and give praise to God except this foreigner?" Then he said to him, "Get up and go on your way; your faith has made you well" (Luke 17:11-19).

A leper came to him begging him, and kneeling he said to him, "If you choose, you can make me clean." Moved with pity, Jesus stretched out his hand and touched him, and said to him, "I do choose. Be made clean!" Immediately the leprosy left him, and he was made clean. After sternly warning him he sent him away at once, saying to him, "See that you say nothing to anyone; but go, show yourself to the priest, and offer for your cleansing what Moses commanded, as a testimony to them" (Mark 1:40-44).

In Old Testament times, according to Leviticus, any person with leprosy, no matter how famous, was "unclean," and to be kept at a distance from others. One of the most famous lepers was Naaman. A man of prominence, "Naaman, commander of the army of the king of Aram, was a great man and in high favour with his master, because by him the Lord had given victory to Aram. The man, though a mighty warrior, suffered from leprosy" (2 Kings 5:1).

In Jesus' day, people who contracted leprosy were victims of discrimination through no fault of their own. They were social outsiders. Their bodies marked with skin lesions that physically disfigured their limbs and eyes, they were subjected to social segregation. They were excluded. They were treated as if their disease defined them. Lumping them together under the term "leper" made it possible to ignore their personalities.

Today, according to the World Health Organization, there are approximately 200,000 people who still suffer from leprosy. Pockets of high vulnerability remain in some areas of Angola, Brazil, Central African Republic, Democratic Republic of Congo, India, Madagascar, Mozambique, Nepal and the United Republic of Tanzania. These countries remain highly committed to eliminating the disease and continue to intensify their leprosy control activities. All the same, even though the debilitating disease is now readily treatable and is not contagious, victims have been and continue to be contained in colonies. Instead of humane treatment they are judged to be socially unfit and sentenced to social isolation. In southern Iraq The Salvation Army had rebuilt a local "leprosy house," and the staff embraced the residents who yearned for a human touch. But when a local TV station sent a film crew to report on the work, they filmed from the road and would not enter the courtyard for fear of the lepers.[1]

Compassion is motivated by empathy. It generates behaviour that sees life from the other person's point of view. True compassion generates responses that open doors for outsiders to become insiders.

The social-outcast scale has numerous levels. Obviously, some experiences of exclusion are more painful and more destructive than others.

Childhood memories can still generate deep feelings in adulthood. Being rejected by your circle of friends, coping with a learning disability, failing a grade at school or always being the last person chosen to make up a sports team can leave emotional scars.

Cultural rejection can be as simple as being born a girl or dealing with the stigma of testing positive for HIV-AIDS. On the religious front, women can be restricted from leadership roles or isolated in separate sections for worship. In some circles, being divorced or living as a lone parent can lead to relational alienation. Doors are often closed in the faces of people having a particular sexual orientation or indulging in certain lifestyle behaviours.

On the outcast scale, the treatment from other people can be more difficult to cope with than carrying the emotional weight of being physically disfigured or mentally challenged.

And then there is the parade of economic disparity. If you are chronically unemployed, a permanent recipient of welfare or live on the street without an address where the government can send you cheques, you can expect "do not enter" signs to be posted at almost every turn.

Identify today's social outsiders

Focus on yourself first
Reach back in your memory to identify a time when you were excluded—an occasion when you were an outsider. Using single words, describe how you felt. Write the words and let them awaken your emotions. Be honest about how they make you feel. Discuss your experience with others.

Your home country
Identify two or three people groups who are excluded—who are outsiders. Be specific and think broadly.

Your church
Identify people who are outsiders. Be honest. They may be tolerated, but are they really welcomed? Again, be specific.

Your global neighbours
Identify at least two people groups who are outsiders. Give attention to those who are subject to stigma and discrimination.

Prayers of Response

Close to home
Our God, we embrace our citizenship as a gift. We acknowledge that we had no choice about where we were born or the kind of families who brought us into this world. Grant us eyes to see those who live among us as outsiders. Protect us from the hardening of our inner spirits that can turn us away from the people who most need us to care. Amen.

Beyond our borders
Creator God, we would like to see ourselves as global citizens. Our intention was never to be imprisoned inside our small worlds. Neither do we desire comfort as our final destination. When opportunities come for us to reach beyond our self-erected borders, help us resist the temptation to stay close to home. Inspire us so we look like we are followers of Jesus. Amen.

Add your own specific prayers for those close to home and those beyond your borders.

Protesting Gender Inequality

The cultural setting in Jesus' day was a tapestry woven of Roman, Greek and Hebrew traditions. There was an intriguing interplay between political power, social customs and religious influences. Although the treatment of women did not equate to the stigma heaped on those who bore the burdens of leprosy, the convergence of Roman, Greek and Hebrew attitudes toward women clearly positioned them as inferior to their male counterparts. Women were second-class, subservient human beings.

Jesus was a social revolutionary and a religious innovator. Jesus included women in his life when other people of influence excluded them. The passages below illustrate how Jesus protested against the gender injustice that swirled around him.

Encountering God in the Biblical Story

Drown out the noise of your distracted mind,
> In quiet reverence be open to receive what God gives you,
> > Prepare yourself to live the salvation story.

- Without commenting, read the three texts below, consecutively and out loud.
- Read the passages a second time. Listen for a word or phrase that catches your attention.
- Meditate on the thought for two to three minutes.
- Share your thought out loud in a simple statement, without elaboration. Listen carefully to each other to see if the comments of others link with your idea.
- Take a few moments to reflect on what you have heard.
- If what someone else observed linked with your observation, comment on how the two ideas reinforce each other.

Now as they went on their way, he entered a certain village, where a woman named Martha welcomed him into her home. She had a sister named Mary, who sat at the Lord's feet and listened to what he was saying. But Martha was distracted by her many tasks; so she came to him and asked, "Lord, do you not care that my sister has left me to do all the work by myself? Tell her then to help me." But the Lord answered her, "Martha, Martha, you are worried and distracted by many things; there is need of only one thing. Mary has chosen the better part, which will not be taken away from her" (Luke 10:38-42).

And Jesus got up and followed him, with his disciples. Then suddenly a woman who had been suffering from hemorrhages for 12 years came up behind him and touched the fringe of his cloak, for she said to herself, "If I only touch his cloak, I will be made well." Jesus turned, and seeing her he said, "Take heart, daughter; your faith has made you well." And instantly the woman was made well. When Jesus came to the leader's house and saw the flute players and the crowd making a commotion, he said, "Go away; for the girl is not dead but sleeping." And they laughed at him. But when the crowd had been put outside, he went in and took her by the hand, and the girl got up. And the report of this spread throughout that district (Matthew 9:19-26).

But Mary stood weeping outside the tomb. As she wept, she bent over to look into the tomb; and she saw two angels in white, sitting where the body of Jesus had been lying, one at the head and the other at the feet. They said to her, "Woman, why are you weeping?" She said to them, "They have taken away my Lord, and I do not know where they have laid him." When she had said this, she turned around and saw Jesus standing there, but she did not know that it was Jesus. Jesus said to her, "Woman, why are you weeping? Whom are you looking for?" Supposing him to be the gardener, she said to him, "Sir, if you have carried him away, tell me where you have laid him, and I will take him away." Jesus said to her, "Mary! She turned and said to him in Hebrew, "Rabbouni!" (which means Teacher). Jesus said to her, "Do not hold on to me, because I have not yet ascended to the Father. But go to my brothers and say to them, 'I am ascending to my Father and your Father, to my God and your God.' " Mary Magdalene went and announced to the disciples, "I have seen the Lord"; and she told them that he had said these things to her (John 20:11-18).

What do these passages teach us about Jesus' views, relationships and practices with women?

• His inner circle of people included women.

- He was approachable—he signalled freedom of access to his time and attention.
- Jesus engaged in candid conversations with the women he knew.
- In response to a parent's pain, there was no discrimination between daughters and sons.
- In her time, the hemorrhaging woman was judged to be unclean. Jesus ignored the ritual purity laws and dignified her in spite of her stigma.
- Outside the tomb in the early morning light, Mary recognized the sound of the voice of Jesus—the voice of the one who had taken time to be her teacher.
- At a most critical time in Christian history, Jesus revealed himself first to a woman.
- In a culture that did not recognize a woman's testimony in a court of law, Jesus trusted Mary to be the first person to spread the Resurrection message.

In Jesus' context, women were considered inferior to men. The New Testament culture was lived in the shadow of Old Testament norms. The legacy of Eve, "the temptress" in the Garden of Eden, lived on. Unmarried women were not allowed to leave the homes of their father. Married women were subject to the decisions of their husbands. Talking to strangers was forbidden. Their testimony in court counted less than that of a man. Women were under the authority of men—more like a possession than a person. Their status was "slave-like" rather than that of dignified human beings. The elevation of Mary, the mother of Jesus, and the inclusion of the Magnificat in Scripture (see Luke 1) stands in contrast with cultural practices of the day.

Many advocates for gender equality would raise their voices and ask, "So what has changed?" They would argue that the subjugation of women is still a problem today. Religious prejudice in favour of men continues to be a reality in some Christian traditions and many churches. Debates continue about "headship" and what ministry roles are allowed for women. Corporate board rooms are populated with majorities of men who retain their power. Even in what we label our "enlightened age," many people continue to believe that a woman's primary role in life is to have children and take care of the home. Even when women are not confined to these roles they still are often trapped with double-duty expectations at work and at home. All the same, compared to Jesus' day, women's rights are surging ahead in many parts of today's world.

Current Challenges

In his time, Jesus elevated women to a new level of life. He bestowed dignity on the female gender in a cultural context where women as a class were repressed and assumed to be inferior. He addressed their injustice with his "let's make life right" behaviour.

In our times, the structures of democratic and secular societies are leading the way in addressing the social injustices faced by women. It is the Universal Declaration of Human Rights, civil rights legislation, employment laws, human rights tribunals and the decisions of the courts that are serving as the primary advocates for gender equality.

The troubling question the people of God face is: If the mission of Jesus on earth in his time is our mission on earth in our time, what attitudes and actions should we express toward women?

Think about specific women in your various relationships and social sectors: family, friends, neighbours, community, church, work, politics, society at large and the global scene. Choose a particular category or two that capture(s) your attention.

- As a woman, what attitudes and actions will address injustice with your "make life right" behaviour?
- As a man, what attitudes and actions will address injustice with your "make life right" behaviour?

Prayers of Response

Close to home
Our Lord, when you lived as we live, you demonstrated the best of life. Our circumstances are not the same but the virtues you

expressed are also meant for us. We confess that neither our world nor our churches have always granted women the equal status they deserve. We confess our prejudices. We lament our readiness to conform to unjust cultural norms when we should have lived differently. And in the midst of the various views we still hold on gender issues, grant us the grace to be respectful of each other. Amen.

Beyond our borders

Our God, we know that being created in your image is more important than whether we are male or female. Tragically, too often we have lived as if it was the other way around. We repent for having been too accepting of social norms that have led to violence against women in our homes. We are ashamed when women are reduced to sexual objects. We have been complacent when HIV-positive mothers do not have the means to protect their newborn babies. Forgive us. And empower us to speak boldly and live bravely. Amen.

Add your own specific prayers for those close to home and those beyond your borders.

Embracing the Excluded

Although Christians around the globe look at Jesus through various lenses, the dominant lens is to view Jesus as "Saviour." He is the Son of God who came to earth and died on the cross to forgive people of their sins and be the Saviour of the world.

In this book, we affirm Jesus as the divine Son of God and, at the same time, we celebrate his humanity as the ultimate expression of how life is best lived. Jesus is both divine and human—a unique and one-time-only revelation. In God's design, the humanity of Jesus is graced with divine presence that makes him sacred and accessible for people everywhere. Regrettably, many who emphasize the divinity of Jesus tend to limit the importance of his humanity. And those who most appreciate his humanity tend to downplay his divinity.

When we embrace Jesus as both divine and human, and seek to understand him through a justice lens, there is a double endorsement. The divinity of Jesus gives authority to his justice teachings and his behavioural practices. And his humanity elevates his life as the example of the best of justice behaviour.

Consequently, when we look at how Jesus treated people with leprosy, women and children, we can understand how God views marginalized people and how they can best be treated in our time. Jesus—showing us how to live and how to love.

Encountering God in the Biblical Story

Orient your spirit in a searching mode,
>> Be attentive in reading,
>>>> Listen for God's voice,
>>>>>> Be faithful in living.

Rather than beginning his Incarnation as a grown adult, Jesus began his life on earth as a baby like the rest of us. His childhood years with Mary, Joseph and the rest of his family bestowed dignity on the ages and stages of children. Later in his life, Jesus was child-friendly. He enjoyed children and blessed them.

- Read the following passages in silence. Read slowly and listen for God's voice.
- Read the passages again out loud.
- Now put yourself into the situations described in the story.
- Describe how the children must have felt.
  ◦ Describe how the disciples and other adults looking on must have felt.
  ◦ In silence, make a mental list of the names of children who come to mind.
- Read the passages again out loud.
- Now, speak the names of children who come to your mind.
- Offer sentence prayers on behalf of the children named.

People were bringing even infants to him that he might touch them; and when the disciples saw it, they sternly ordered them not to do it. But Jesus called for them and said, "Let the little children come to me, and do not stop them; for it is to such as these that the kingdom of God belongs. Truly I tell you, whoever does not receive the kingdom of God as a little child will never enter it" (Luke 18:15-17).

At that time the disciples came to Jesus and asked, "Who is the greatest in the kingdom of heaven?" He called a child, whom he put among them, and said, "Truly I tell you, unless you change and become like children, you will never enter the kingdom of heaven. Whoever becomes humble like this child is the greatest in the kingdom of heaven. Whoever welcomes one such child in my name welcomes me. If any of you put a stumbling block before one of these little ones who believe in me, it would be better for you if a great millstone were fastened around your neck and you were drowned in the depth of the sea. Woe to the world because of stumbling blocks! Occasions for stumbling are bound to come, but woe to the one by whom the stumbling block comes! (Matthew 18:1-7).

People in New Testament times were as influenced by the norms of culture as we are by ours. And in Jesus' day, the culture and customs were blatantly patriarchal. Men ruled on all fronts. As heads of households, men made the decisions. If husbands didn't have the only word, they had the final word. The authority of fathers was unquestioned. Sons were far more significant than daughters, especially as the first-born child in a family.

Of course, children were still loved by their families. Brothers and sisters played games and argued with each other. They raced and wrestled. They giggled and cried as children do. But as children, they were subjected to the cultural practices of the day. There was a utilitarian set of assumptions. Wives were to fulfill the function of producing a male heir for the husband. Children were expected to provide economic support for the family. They were the social safety net for parents in their old age.

Childhood was a stage of life to be obedient to parents and prepare to become responsible adults. Children were not invited to dream about what they could become. Beyond participation in their families, children were socially insignificant. They were cultural nobodies. Their voices didn't count. Consequently, when the Bible reports that Jesus miraculously fed 5,000, the women and the children were excluded from the count.

Current Challenges

Jesus treats children with respect. Rather than excluding them, Jesus embraces them. Rather than pushing them to the edges of life as his male disciples wanted, Jesus brings children to the centre stage.

Jesus chides his disciples: "Let the children teach you. Don't exclude them. Learn from them." "Truly I tell you, whoever does not receive the kingdom of God as a little child will never enter it." "Truly I tell you, unless you change and become like children, you will never enter the kingdom of heaven."

- What is Jesus teaching us here? In what ways should we be like children in order to be welcomed into God's kingdom— God's family?

Children are fragile and vulnerable. Jesus warns us to protect them, and in particular not to be "stumbling blocks." There are consequences if we lead them astray.

- In their relationships with adults, what obstacles and stumbling blocks do children face? How can adults lead children astray?
- Thinking about the needs of children, what protections do children need from adults in these times?
- Complete the sentence: "People who champion children
_____."

At present more than a half million students are enrolled in Salvation Army schools, most of them in junior grades and almost all of them in less-developed countries. For those who attend, this means life-long doors of opportunity are opened. But what of those who can't? Even modest fees for tuition and school uniforms exclude millions of the world's children from the classroom. What prospects do they have?

Prayers of Response

Close to home
Our Father, we come to you as your children. As followers of Jesus, we are thankful to be a part of your extended family. We all cherish memories from the experiences of our earthly families. Some of us were smothered with over-protective love. Others of us spent too many days and nights feeling unloved. Whatever our past, we have high aspirations for today's generation of children. May they live in places where they are loved, where they are safe, where they are free to play and challenged to learn. And may they also know that they are both treasured and loved by you. Amen.

Beyond our borders
Our God, we pray for the children of the world. Grant your protection to those who live in the squalor of garbage dumps and to the little ones who are cushioned in privilege. They all need to be loved. But especially, give your attention to those who live with little food, to those who lack access to safe water and adequate health care. Extend your mercy to those who are forced to go to work instead of going to

school. And please God, walk closely with the children who live with the injustice of having to be parents to their younger brothers and sisters. Amen.

Add your own specific prayers for those close to home and those beyond your borders.

The Salvation Army Story: Valuing Everyone's Gifts

There is no longer Jew or Greek, there is no longer slave or free, there is no longer male and female; for all of you are one in Christ Jesus (Galatians 3:28).

Women in England in the 1850s had limited status. They were barred from higher education. They had no vote. Their financial power was marginal. The expectation was that they would be subservient to men anywhere the genders mixed.

In churches, leadership roles were firmly closed to women. There were sacred rules that said so. But it wasn't just the *rules* that kept women from being preachers and teachers. Prejudicial attitudes meant the rules generally went unquestioned. It's hard for us to fathom now, but people found it *funny* when Samuel Johnston said, "A woman's preaching is like a dog's walking on his hind legs. It is not done well; but you are surprised to find it done at all"!

This is the world into which Catherine Mumford, who later became Catherine Booth, was born.

Thankfully, God gifted her with a capacity to understand the Bible for herself and the courage to speak up in her time and place. As Catherine Mumford Booth understood the Bible, salvation in Jesus meant the effects of the fall were to be reversed here and now. Redemption ushered in a new creation. In gender matters, whatever "curse" had befallen women was undone in the victory of Jesus over sin. Men that undermined the gender equality that had been God's original intention were to be challenged.

For Catherine, the Scriptures ruled. The prophet Joel claimed that in "those days" the Holy Spirit would come and gift women as well as men to "prophesy." The Apostle Peter declared that "those days" were fully endorsed by the Resurrection of Jesus.

To Catherine, "those days" meant that God the Spirit was gifting women for public ministry. Accordingly, individuals or structures that tried to silence women's voices in public were wrong. The "shall" of Joel inscribed in the Book of Acts is not only a prescription for men. Women also *shall* prophesy.

God was speaking to more women than just Catherine. In the late 1850s, an American holiness preacher, Phoebe Palmer, was on tour in England. Immersed in their gender biases, some local ministers condemned Phoebe in print and tried to stop their parishioners from attending her meetings. Catherine's response was to pen a 32-page pamphlet—"Female Ministry; or, Woman's Right to Preach the Gospel"—which became a landmark document in the emancipation of women. Her proclamation endures:

> "If this passage [Galatians 3:28] does not teach
> that in the privileges, duties, and responsibilities
> of Christ's kingdom, all differences of nation, caste
> and sex are abolished, we should like to know
> what it does teach, and wherefore it was written."[2]

When Catherine wrote these words, she had no aspirations to be a preacher or church leader. (She never was a Salvation Army officer and her preaching ministry only came later.) The pamphlet was an act of advocacy to defend *other* women who were being excluded and belittled on the basis of prejudice and errant theology.

The arguments penned in 1859 had long-term structural implications. Catherine's convictions resulted in gender equality being part of the constitution of the Christian Mission and subsequently one of the core principles of The Salvation Army. If historians are right, equal opportunity is one reason many women were attracted to The Salvation Army.

We continue to be aware that Catherine Booth's convictions have not convinced *everybody*. By insisting that the gifts of the Spirit be recognized in a gender-neutral way, The Salvation Army itself has experienced exclusion and sometimes been made to sit on the ecumenical sidelines. For women to have served communion would have been a scandal among 19th-century Anglicans. And while many Anglican churches have progressed in their gender practices and even surpassed The Salvation Army, there are other members of the

Christian church for whom the ordination of women is still a battleground.

But let's be honest. The early positioning of women in The Salvation Army has still not found its full implementation. Is this because the Holy Spirit has not been gifting women in our century? Or is that social convention has made us reticent to recognize what the Spirit has given us?

The point is not to establish gender or racial quotas or any other mathematical meaning of recognition. Being "one in Christ" bestows equal value on both genders. Inclusion is to honour God and honour people as gifts God has given for the purpose of mobilizing the church for the transformation of creation. Whether it's a Catherine Booth or anyone else, silencing someone whom the Spirit has gifted to speak, overlooking anyone whom the Spirit has gifted to serve, immobilizes us all. A gift not recognized is a gift not freed for mission, and a gift not freed for mission is a gift wasted.

Imagine the impact on the world when there is a Salvation Army in which "there is no longer Jew or Greek, there is no longer slave or free, there is no longer male and female; for all ... are one in Christ Jesus" (Galatians 3:28).

~~~~

A case can be made that inclusion of both women and men is a prerequisite of the gospel. Equal regard for both sexes is consistent with Jesus' measure of justice. But to many the absence of equality and inclusion in today's world does not appear to be alarming. When we look outward to our fractured world, social caste systems pervade, inequalities are obvious and the triumph of power of one over another is often celebrated.

The Salvation Army Kate Booth House, where I was stationed in Vancouver, never fully knew what would be ushered through the back door. Picture the day a woman and child entered, holding on to each other for dear life. The little one was brought to mingle with similar victims in the new children's play area. Having been treated abusively and deprived of food, the young mom found herself at our dining room table. The victim of monstrous injustice, her swollen black and blue face meant she had been used as a punching bag.

A curious five-year-old child who had already lived at Kate Booth House for a period of time invited herself to a seat at the table directly across from the newcomer. Our worker stared in the child's direction with eyes that read, "Don't you dare make a comment!" Oblivious to the concern, the curious child opened her mouth with words that only heaven could have sent. "Oh, what beautiful hair you have!" In that moment, heaven and earth kissed, lighting the room with intrusive love. The bruised and swollen face, so long wreathed in darkness, broke into a smile.

When Galatians 3:28 is lived, no one is excluded from the family reunion. In God's providence, some expressions of love are sealed tight in unnamed envelopes. And when they are opened, healing begins its journey. That day, the envelope that had been sealed shut with the secrets of domestic violence was broken open. A battered mom was included at the table and invited to join the Kate Booth House family.

If five-year-olds can find unprecedented ways to include the excluded, imagine what the rest of us can do.—MCM

~~~

Gifts do not have to be large or showy to be valuable. That is proved by a story told by Paul du Plessis about the time when he was the assistant chief medical officer at the 250-bed Salvation Army hospital in Zambia.

One of the patients in the leprosarium was Rebecca Mutanti. The advance of her disease had left her with loss of feeling in her hands and feet. Her hands were fingerless. Her facial deformity was obvious. It was easy to see why the fears of fellow villagers had created stigma and enforced isolation. On the bright side, her facial deformity did not rob her of a radiant smile.

When Rebecca, already the head of the Women's Village, was appointed home league secretary, Paul's wife, Margaret du Plessis, became her assistant. They got together for planning the weekly meetings. Margaret taught Rebecca and the women dress-making skills. Rebecca taught Margaret how to cook Zambian style.

The relationship began to bridge language, racial and cultural differences. Mutual respect was growing. Then when Margaret and Paul lost their five-day-old son in 1971, the mission staff seemed at a loss to know how to support them. Rebecca appeared at the du Plessis' back door with a few coins from her meagre earnings in her palms. She just sat there in silence with a grieving mother.

Small gestures defined a personal relationship. The major gifts Rebecca and Margaret exchanged were gifts of respect and hospitality. Observed by others, their relationship opened the door to further changes. Each year when it came to the Women's World Day of Prayer in that area of Zambia, congregations met together—except, of course, the women from the Leprosy Settlement Corps. Those with the dreaded disease simply accepted their rejection. Then in God's mercy, the home league secretary from the nearby corps approached Margaret and asked, "Do you think the women from the Leprosy Settlement Corps would be willing to join us? We've been watching you and other missionaries relate to those with leprosy over these years, and we think it would be good to invite them." Heaven's angels surely rejoiced that day.

~~~~

There was no rejoicing about what I discovered after receiving an invitation to spend time in Mexico. I was the weekend guest speaker. With an audience of Salvationists, we exchanged ideas and sang our songs. On the Sunday night it was suggested that Monday could be a tourist day. A trip outside the city to visit historical sights of global renown and eat together with the leaders was a pleasant thought. I was comfortable with the plan until I overheard a conversation that made me decide Monday's schedule had to be altered. I discovered that there were Salvation Army officers and lay people from their congregation who regularly made their way into the city at night with food and a desire to care for people and build relationships. I asked if I could change my schedule and be included.

We adjusted our tourist excursion to get back in time for a foray into the city. Our first stop was the Salvation Army corps, where we loaded the vehicle with soup and bread. I was told simply that we would meet homeless people. To my surprise, we began making our way into secret places—city dwellings hidden behind vegetation and vacant lots. When we arrived, people came out to us for the soup. Members of the corps who had been there before led us into the crooks and crevices of the landscape.

That night, I talked with teenage mothers and held little babies who were attempting to survive in a nation where the social fabric did not include resources for their needs. And then our conversation turned to what, for me, remains unforgettable.

There were more hidden areas we could not reach. To my horror, the ground under our feet had a network of sewers where hundreds of kids lived. Just blocks away there were those who lived up top with their ample houses and well-manicured gardens. Parents there had children, too, and naturally were concerned about their well-being. On occasion, these well-cared-for children took ill and required an organ transplant. That night I learned a solution to the crisis could be had for a price. A sewer kid would be kidnapped by people in an unmarked vehicle. The system was in place for a payment to be made in exchange for a kidney or any other organ on the purchase list. Children were smuggled into the operating room where the theft of their life resource was perpetrated. The organ was trafficked across the hallway to a family waiting with anticipation. Then, just two or three days later, the "donor" would be taken back to their "address" to re-enter their sewer domain, weak and helpless.

Secrets live in the sewers of injustice. Children whose names are not known—excluded from the city census as if they simply don't exist. —MCM

~~~~

When you are a social worker you are prone to label your world according to categories. You are a professional who is taught to diagnose situations and identify others by the names of their circumstances—"homeless," "mentally ill," "hungry," "poor," "trafficked." People's real names given at birth can remain unknown along with the stories of their lives.

Never knowing the names of the "categorized" and living with indifference to reasons for their plight is another form of exclusion.

My vocational tradition uses titles that signal upward mobility and positions of accomplishment. Positions with credentials and career promotions can be places to hide. Closed office doors with name plates that signal increased positional power can become places that exclude people. God help us to transcend the temptations to label people or use our job ranking to exclude the people we should know by name.

In a speaking series one Easter weekend, I shared Mary's encounter with Jesus in his post-resurrected state as recorded in John 20. Mary hears Jesus call her by name. What a moment that must have been. Mary is recognized and validated by hearing her birth name. After being called "Commissioner" all weekend, on Sunday morning I shared with the congregation that there is nothing like being called by your first name. As I shook hands with members of the congregation at the end of the service, some dared to greet me by "Christine." I sensed a childlike warmth of engagement as we stepped off our pedestals of exclusion.—MCM

~~~~

God's vision of Galatians 3:28 is still unfinished.

"Inclusion" and "exclusion" are not descriptive words; they are value words. They are measures of both justice and injustice. Our world remains scarred until the categories that describe our humanity are not marred by superiority and segregation. Our societies are less than they are meant to be until the neglected children and vulnerable mothers are protected. Our lives together are blemished until our worth is found in who we are rather than what we do.

CHAPTER 2

CHALLENGING CULTURAL PRACTICES

He has told you, O mortal, what is good;
and what does the Lord require of you
but to do justice, and to love kindness,
and to walk humbly with your God?
(Micah 6:8)

Let right relationships mark your days and nights.
Walk humbly with God,
    Offer gifts of mercy to friends and neighbours,
    Seek justice for those treated unfairly.
Let God be God so you can know how to assess yourself,
    Choose kindness when tempted to lash out,
    Pursue what's right for those who have been wronged.
Allow God to direct your paths,
    Extend the benefit of the doubt to others.
    Spend your social influence for the sake of those who have
no influence—
    Challenge society instead of blaming the victims.

Justice is a concept with many meanings. It is too multi-dimensional to be reduced to a single dictionary definition.

There is *legal/courtroom justice:* In democratic societies and many other cultures there is an assumption that "you get what you deserve." Virtue is rewarded, evil is punished and criminals are brought to justice. They are penalized according to the law as guilty offenders. The justice system holds court and penalties are meted out to fit the crime.

There is *ethical/human-rights justice:* Ethical justice gives a different meaning to "you get what you deserve." In the moral equation that links basic rights with being a human being, individuals are inherently worthy to have a place in society and to contribute to and receive benefits from their society. Citizens thereby have rights to education, health care and opportunities for employment that make human flourishing possible. A society is a "just society" when equitable access to the advantages and benefits of the nation are available to all. Social-justice advocates contend that these same human rights and equality principles should be extended to all global citizens.

Then, there is *divine justice/God's justice:* God's justice embraces measures of both legal and ethical justice. In some senses, people who disregard God's laws of life get their "just deserts." Sin generates its inevitable swath of destruction. Selfishness eventually inflicts its punishment. Unrestrained greed guarantees disgrace and even revenge from those who have been exploited. Deceit may lead to short-term gain but guarantees long-term pain.

In another sense, however, the spiritual paradox of God's justice is that we don't get "what we deserve." Instead of punishment, we receive forgiveness. Rather than being forever guilty, we are granted a clean slate—a kind of clemency. And then, we are invited to walk alongside Jesus, who has already shown us how to live and how to love. As people who are forgiven and loved, God enables us to live right and participate in making life right with others.

But how do we participate in seeking God's justice? What's the Christian motivation?

First of all, we recognize the value of every human being. We accept the Christian conviction that every person is created in the image of God. Every person—no exceptions—is marked with God's beauty. And consequently, every person is to be treasured and treated justly.

The second mandate is to be motivated by love—the practice of loving one's neighbour as oneself. When we are at our best, God's love in us knows no limits. And the God-given capacity to love generates right relationships—relationships that include a vision to protect the vulnerable.

Divine justice is generated by God's love. The expanse of God's love incorporates justice. The tenacity of God's love let loose in the human spirit refuses to accept injustice. Pursuing justice becomes part of what it means to love.

God's justice invites us into the spiritual equation that lifts life above the level of merely legal and ethical justice. We are participants with the worldwide body of Christ, envisioning a just creation—a world where people are living with equal dignity, equal rights and equal respect—in right relationship with each other.

Accordingly, we imagine, we dream, we pray, we work for a world where we—

> Live equal—without discrimination.
> Live safe—without violence.
> Live fair—without exploitation.
> We live with choices.
> We live with dignity.
> We live with mercy.
> We eliminate inequities.
> We embrace opportunities to learn and work.
> We advocate.
> We live forgiven and extend forgiveness to others.
> We live being loved in right relationships.
> We hunger and thirst for justice for all.

Rejecting Racism

Racism is a life-denying force, a weapon of injustice. It is a "sin structure" that denies people opportunities to stand as equals. Racism demeans its victims and vetoes their true humanity. Its abusive power condemns people to ethnic prisons and social-class ghettos. Racism locks the doors to desirable employment, limits relationships and consigns people to economic impoverishment. In history's darkest hours, racism has generated death squads and justified "ethnic cleansing" and genocide. And although we cannot allow ourselves to countenance such horrors, if we are honest, there are traces of this life-denying disease in all of us. We silently feel that we are superior to someone somewhere based on our race, nationality, culture or personal pride.

Encountering God in the Biblical Story

> *Acknowledge we can resist God's will and ways,*
> *Confess that we are influenced by the culture around us,*
> *Permit knowledge to evangelize our behaviour,*
> *Allow mystery to capture our attention.*

- Read the story silently, focusing on the dynamics between Jesus and the woman.
- Read the story again, this time audibly. Imagine yourself as an on-site observer. Listen carefully to the dialogue between the woman and Jesus.
- Resisting the temptation to spiritualize the encounter, attempt to get inside the feelings of the Samaritan woman. Reflect on her self-image as she arrived at the well, then ponder the impact of the event on the woman and attempt to describe the feelings she must have had as she left Jesus and walked away from the well.
- If you could hear the woman's inner thoughts as she walked down the road, what do you think she would have said to herself?
- If you are working with a group, compare your insights and comments with the others.

Jesus left Judea and started back to Galilee. But he had to go through Samaria. So he came to a Samaritan city called Sychar, near the plot of ground that Jacob had given to his son Joseph. Jacob's well was there, and Jesus, tired out by his journey, was sitting by the well. It was about noon.

A Samaritan woman came to draw water, and Jesus said to her, "Give me a drink."(His disciples had gone to the city to buy food.) The Samaritan woman said to him, "How is it that you, a Jew, ask a drink of me, a woman of Samaria?" (Jews do not share things in common with Samaritans.) Jesus answered her, "If you knew the gift of God, and who it is that is saying to you, 'Give me a drink,' you would have asked him, and he would have given you living water." The woman said to him, "Sir, you have no bucket, and the well is deep. Where do you get that living water? Are you greater than our ancestor Jacob, who gave us the well, and with his sons and his flocks drank from it?" Jesus said to her, "Everyone who drinks of this water will be thirsty again, but those who drink of the water that I will give them will never be thirsty. The water that I will give will become in them a spring of water gushing up to eternal life." The woman said to him, "Sir, give me this water, so that I may never be thirsty or have to keep coming here to draw water."

Jesus said to her, "Go, call your husband, and come back." The woman answered him, "I have no husband." Jesus said to her, "You are right in saying, 'I have no husband'; for you have had five husbands, and the one you have now is not your husband. What you have said is true!" The woman said to him, "Sir, I see that you are a prophet. Our ancestors worshipped on this mountain, but you say that the place where people must worship is in Jerusalem." Jesus said to her, "Woman, believe me, the hour is coming when you will worship the Father neither on this mountain nor in Jerusalem. You worship what you do not know; we worship what we know, for salvation is from the Jews. But the hour is coming, and is now here, when the true worshippers will worship the Father in spirit and truth, for the Father seeks such as these to worship him. God is spirit, and those who worship him must worship in spirit and truth." The woman said to him, "I know that Messiah is coming" (who is called Christ). "When he comes, he will proclaim all things to us." Jesus said to her, "I am he, the one who is speaking to you."

Just then his disciples came. They were astonished that he was speaking with a woman, but no one said, "What do you want?" or, "Why are you speaking with her?" Then the woman left her water jar and went back to the city. She said to the people, "Come and see a man who told me everything I have ever done! He cannot be the Messiah, can he?" They left the city and were on their way to him.

Meanwhile the disciples were urging him, "Rabbi, eat something." But he said to them, "I have food to eat that you do not know about." So the disciples said to one another, "Surely no one has brought him something to eat?" Jesus said to them, "My food is to do the will of him who sent me and to complete his work. Do you not say, 'Four months more, then comes the harvest'? But I tell you, look around you, and see how the fields are ripe for harvesting. The reaper is already receiving wages and is gathering fruit for eternal life, so that sower and reaper may rejoice together. For here the saying holds true, 'One sows and another reaps.' I sent you to reap that for which you did not labour. Others have laboured, and you have entered into their labour."

Many Samaritans from that city believed in him because of the woman's testimony, "He told me everything I have ever done." So when the Samaritans came to him, they asked him to stay with them; and he stayed there two days. And many more believed because of his word. They said to the woman, "It is no longer because of what you said that we believe, for we have heard for ourselves, and we know that this is truly the Saviour of the world" (John 4:1-42).

In Jesus' day, expressions of racism were both overt and approved. Samaritans were the recipients of the prejudice and discrimination. They lived in the region of Samaria, the land of the ancient northern kingdom of Israel that had been conquered centuries prior to the birth of Jesus. In Jewish lore, the Samaritans were the offspring of intermarriages of Assyrians and Israelites. They were looked upon as "half breeds"—a mongrel mix of ethnic impurity. Consequently, they were culturally cut off from those who were ethnically "pure." The social fallout generated mutual animosity between the Jews and Samaritans.[3]

Jesus understood the prevailing cultural practices—the stereotyping and the segregation. The unnamed Samaritan woman whom Jesus encountered at Jacob's well knew it, too. "How is it that you, a Jew, ask a drink of me, a woman of Samaria?" she asked. Still, in one purposeful, but quiet, move toward her, Jesus countered culture and broke the barriers of both racial bigotry and gender discrimination.

Current Challenges

Class-structure superiority pervades the human landscape. The sense of being superior is most often triggered when we compare ourselves to others and we think "I'm better than you." The triggering points include family history, economic standing, intelligence levels, educational achievement, occupation status, spiritual maturity, social skills, skin colour and ethnicity. Identify one or two of the triggering points where, if you are honest, you are vulnerable to feeling superior to others. Why do you think you feel that way? How does feeling superior affect your behaviour? What do you think you can do to alter your attitudes and vulnerability?

The Samaritan woman began the day with a tarnished reputation. Later in the day she was the talk of the town in a different way. What do you think the townspeople said about her following her encounter with Jesus? If you had listened in on the disciples' conversation over their evening meal, what comments do you think you would have heard?

The Holocaust, the killing fields of Cambodia, the Rwandan genocide, the Darfur scandal and other racially-motivated horrors have disgraced our human landscape and marred God's creation in the last hundred years.

The Salvation Army itself complied with the apartheid regime of South Africa before 1991. If silence and disengagement are not options in these situations, what can we do? Individually? Collectively? Here's what The Salvation Army said in its confession to South Africa's Truth and Reconciliation Commission: "While we did care for body and soul, we ought more strongly to have attacked the evil which wrecked both bodies and souls in the first place. Professing an apolitical stance, we used this to avoid the kind of protest for which the early Salvation Army was known." The statement went on to commit The Salvation Army "to following through on the reconciliation process, to a balancing of the priestly and prophetic roles in ministry, to the just redistribution of resources in South Africa and to continue to offer pastoral care to the victims and perpetrators of apartheid-era crimes."[4]

Prayers of Response

Close to home

Our God, we want to proclaim our innocence. Pleading guilty to the "racist" label is too heavy a burden to bear. But, when we are strong enough to be honest with our own souls, we confess that we have been stained. In our silence, we have looked at others and thought, "I am better than you are; my kind, my tribe is superior to yours." Lord, instil in us a yearning for what is right, for what is good, for what is just. Amen.

Beyond our borders

Creator God, why is it easier to be exclusive than inclusive? Why do we defend our disruptive behaviour through the screen of our good intentions while we judge the behaviour of others by their unruly actions? Why is it easier to condemn ethnic violence in countries far away from our national borders than it is to confess the social atrocities inside our own nation? Lord, we are less than we can be, more self-absorbed than we are meant to be, more ethnocentric than is good for our shared world. We need your spirit to intervene. Amen.

Add your own specific prayers for those close to home and those beyond your borders.

Dignifying Second-Class Citizens

Who is my neighbour?" is a troublesome and complex question. The neighbour dilemma is especially thorny when it is linked to justice issues that involve a sense of responsibility for other people's predicaments. The encounter between Jesus and the lawyer that prompted the parable of the Good Samaritan is a starting place for us to unravel the complexities.

Encountering God in the Biblical Story

If you are working with a group, pray together:

God, enlighten our memories to avoid errors from the past,
Enliven our consciences to do what is right in the present,
Shape our character to guide our conduct in the future.

Involve three people, with one as the moderator, to read the connecting phrases in the text. Identify a second person in the group to read the lawyer's script and another person to read the words of Jesus.

Listen carefully as the text is read out loud.

- Without responding, take time to reflect in silence.
- Have the three people re-read the encounter. As they do so, identify one observation to share with the group.
- Share your observations with each other.

Just then a lawyer stood up to test Jesus. "Teacher," he said, "what must I do to inherit eternal life?" He said to him, "What is written in the Law? What do you read there?" He answered, "You shall love the Lord your God with all your heart, and with all your soul, and with all your strength, and with all your mind; and your neighbour as yourself." And he said to him, "You have given the right answer; do this, and you will live."

But wanting to justify himself, he asked Jesus, "And who is my neighbour?" Jesus replied, "A man was going down from Jerusalem to Jericho, and fell into the hands of robbers, who stripped him, beat him, and went away, leaving him half dead. Now by chance a priest was going down that road; and when he saw him, he passed by on the other side. So likewise a Levite, when he came to the place and saw him, passed by on the other side. But a Samaritan while travelling came near him; and when he saw him, he was moved with pity. He went to him and bandaged his wounds, having poured oil and wine on them. Then he put him on his own animal, brought him to an inn, and took care of him. The next day he took out two denarii, gave them to the innkeeper, and said, 'Take care of him; and when I come back, I will repay you whatever more you spend.' Which of these three, do you think, was a neighbour to the man who fell into the hands of the robbers?" He said, "The one who showed him mercy." Jesus said to him, "Go and do likewise" (Luke 10:25-37).

History offers us many reasons to celebrate, but it is also marked with a lack of neighbourliness that has scarred our humanity with exploitation and abuse. The slave trade is a reminder of how racist and cruel people can be toward "the other."

Jesus lived in a class-structure culture where discrimination was rampant and thought to be normal. Religious leaders were part of an elite class structure. Full participation in temple and synagogue life was restricted to the members of one ethnic family. Samaritans were victims of ethnic discrimination. And in the midst of that social milieu, Jesus was a cultural disrupter.

During his years of ministry, Jesus attained some social prominence. There was countryside talk about this new prophet. His teaching caused a stir. His miracles made headlines. Messiah rumours began to circulate. Jesus was more careful and calculating than in previous days. And again, he can be found in a public forum, this time interacting with a lawyer.

In the biblical account, it is the lawyer who asks the first question, "Teacher, what must I do to inherit eternal life?" Jesus fields the question with a two-part response. "What is written in the Law? What do you read there?" Taking the bait and seeing an opportunity to parade his knowledge of Scripture, the lawyer recites the right answer. Displaying keen intellect, the lawyer and Jesus continue their verbal sparring. Jesus then seizes the situation for a remarkable teaching moment by telling a story.

The impact of the parable is profound. Jesus' own people are the target audience. His cultural inheritance makes him fully aware of the ethnic tension between the Jewish people and the Samaritans. He turns the prevailing social status upside down. The upper-caste priests and the Levite temple custodians are portrayed as the villains. The inferior-caste Samaritans are applauded for their superior moral behaviour.

The words of Jesus liberate the Samaritans from their second-class status. His parable confronts racial prejudice, elevates the marginalized and endorses religious practices outside of temple rituals. In a radical fashion, the doors to the community of faith are opened to more than just one ethnic people. The prevailing notion that God loves one race or class more than another is defeated. Jesus' actions announce that all peoples are chosen and loved by God. The cultural and ethnic containment of faith is shattered. The encounter is a mighty blow to the cultural status quo.

Current Challenges

Let's be clear. In both Old Testament and New Testament terms, "loving your neighbour as yourself" is not about cultivating the art of reciprocal living. The "you scratch my back, I'll scratch yours" maxim doesn't qualify. If you invite me to your house for dinner and I reciprocate by inviting you to my house, I still fall short. Instead, it is helpful for us to define neighbours with an external viewfinder. Specifically, neighbours are *"anyone within reach of our 'make a difference' compassion."* Neighbours are not just anyone from anywhere. They are people within tangible reach of our compassion. The challenge from Jesus is to realize how widely our compassion can reach.

- *Look closely*: Understand "neighbours" as people you know by name. Start with family and extend to friends. Draw the circle to include people who live nearby, colleagues in your work-place and church community. Extend the reach to relationships that had meaning in the past and be ready to respond to those who are yet to appear in your life.

- *Reach beyond self-interest*: Self-interest-only living is for whiners. If the parable of the Good Samaritan teaches us anything, it is that self-interest is exchanged for the best interests of the other. The Christian meaning of neighbour turns our eyes and ears outward.
- *Do something global*: When the pursuit of justice is linked with the vision Jesus had for living right and making life right with others, loving our global neighbours is non-negotiable. Global neighbours are informed. They pray intelligently, give money strategically, defend human rights and advocate for justice beyond their national borders.
- *Don't get superior*: Generous neighbours risk believing the giving is all on their side. The truth is that to be human is to be dependent, and would-be benefactors often find themselves to have received more than they gave. Do not forget to show hospitality to strangers, for by so doing some people have shown hospitality to angels without knowing it (see Hebrews 13:2).

The Island of Goree is situated a few kilometres off the shoreline of Dakar, Senegal, in West Africa. Today, the island is a tourist attraction that features the architecture of Portuguese, Dutch and French conquerors. But historically, Goree was a slave-trade prison compound. It was one of the transit centres where black African captives were gathered and locked up until they were shipped off to the New World. Those who survived the journey became commodities to serve the economic interests of plantation owners and other people with social power.

In some ways, things are very different today. In 2008, the United States elected a gifted black man as its president. But when you connect the cultural dots to the events of history, consequences still prevail. Walk the streets of Savannah, Georgia, and observe the painful effects of the legacy from the past. Hotel managers are white and service staff is African American. Business owners are white and cashiers are black. Most often the wealthy are white and the poor are black. Tourists are invited to tour plantations to see how life used to be, but it is all too evident that in many ways the class structure and the discrimination of the past continue.

In other "developed" countries, the historical and cultural struggle of indigenous people groups continues. Aboriginal Peoples in Canada, Australia and South American countries struggle daily with discrimination and repression. According to the law they may be equal, but in reality they live as second-class citizens.

- Think about your neighbours. Write down names and identify people in three categories: 1) People close by—people you know by name; 2) People you sometimes think about—people you read about or hear about on television; people who used to live close to you but have moved away; people who catch your attention in difficult situations; people who live beyond your self-interest but keep entering your awareness; 3) Global neighbours—people in countries who sometimes capture your long-distance interest and compassion. Choose a person who is struggling. Identify a situation that arouses your compassion. Decide to do something tangible to express your concern.
- Responding to the needs of neighbours is inconvenient and it can be costly. "Loving your neighbour" involves the precious currencies of both time and money. Paradoxically, it is often the case that people who have time do not have money and those with money often lack time. Which currency do you value more? Between time and money, which is easier for you to release?
- Reflect on the culture in which you live. Identify people groups—particularly second-class citizens who are subjected to social, sexual or religious stigma. What expressions of "good neighbour" behaviour will put a smile on their faces? What initiatives can lead to their social benefit?

- Jesus' parable focuses on individual care. The victim is rescued by the Samaritan. A deeper look reveals systemic social structures affecting the behaviour of the priest and the Levite. Identify organizations that work with some of the people groups you named in the previous question. Don't restrict yourself to Salvation Army ministries, but don't assume you already know everything about those ministries either. Invite a representative to present their work to your group; make an appointment to visit their offices; consider becoming a volunteer and joining their causes.

Prayers of Response

Close to home

Living God, as your people, we are your hands, your feet, your lips, your cheque-writers. We are your co-creators. We know that when we love, we are alive. We have learned that we are most alive when we love. And you have made it clear that our love for you and our love for our neighbours are inseparable. Energize us to live your love in ways that opens doors of opportunities for people who struggle on the edges. Enable us to unwrap ourselves for the sake of others. Amen.

Beyond our borders

Creator God, we recognize that some countries are less developed than others. The reasons are many, but some nations are more prosperous and people who live in them are more privileged. We pray that our government and business decision makers will be good Samaritans. May their actions be marked with generosity. Whether the issue is trade tariffs, gifts in kind, medical patents, money or accessing the latest technology, may the world's more-developed countries share their bounty with those nations who live with so much less. Amen.

Add your own specific prayers for those close to home and those beyond your borders.

Risking One's Reputation

Jesus' equation for living fully is startling:

> Express love for God, yourself and others and you will live;
> Refuse to express love for God, yourself and others and you
> will die.

In other words, living without loving is like committing suicide in slow motion. And the premise of this series of studies is that Jesus does not just teach solid theory, but his life expresses best how to live and love. Jesus repeatedly demonstrates that seeking justice for the other is an expression of love.

We may not be surprised to see Jesus defend Samaritans and lobby for the dignity of those who are excluded from main-street living. However, we are inclined to take a second look when we see Jesus spending time with prostitutes and drunkards. Having compassion for people who live in sin is one matter, but inviting them into his circle of friends is shocking (see Luke 7:34). Then again, his actions are only surprising until we look more closely at his overall approach to people. Jesus reached out repeatedly beyond the norms of social convention. His love for his neighbours extended to *anyone within reach of his "make-a-difference" compassion.*

Encountering God in the Biblical Story

> *Let God's grace draw you close,*
> *Let God's truth inspire you,*
> *Let God's love excite you.*

- Read the three texts consecutively in silence and without comment.
- Have someone read the texts a second time out loud. Focus on how Jesus related to the tax collectors and women.
- Read the text a third time, again out loud. This time, focus on how Jesus responded to the Pharisees in the texts.
- Write down your primary impressions.
- Discuss your impressions with each other.

As Jesus was walking along, he saw a man called Matthew sitting at the tax booth; and he said to him, "Follow me." And he got up and followed him.

And as he sat at dinner in the house, many tax collectors and sinners came and were sitting with him and his disciples. When the Pharisees saw this, they said to his disciples, "Why does your teacher eat with tax collectors and sinners?" But when he heard this, he said, "Those who are well have no need of a physician, but those who are sick. Go and learn what this means, 'I desire mercy, not sacrifice.' For I have come to call not the righteous but sinners" (Matthew 9:9-13) .

One of the Pharisees asked Jesus to eat with him, and he went into the Pharisee's house and took his place at the table. And a woman in the city, who was a sinner, having learned that he was eating in the Pharisee's house, brought an alabaster jar of ointment. She stood behind him at his feet, weeping, and began to bathe his feet with her tears and to dry them with her hair. Then she continued kissing his feet and anointing them with the ointment. Now when the Pharisee who had invited him saw it, he said to himself, "If this man were a prophet, he would have known who and what kind of woman this is who is touching him—that she is a sinner." Jesus spoke up and said to him, "Simon, I have something to say to you." "Teacher," he replied, "speak." "A certain creditor had two debtors; one owed 500 denarii, and the other 50. When they could not pay, he cancelled the debts for both of them. Now which of them will love him more?" Simon answered, "I suppose the one for whom he cancelled the greater debt." And Jesus said to him, "You have judged rightly." Then turning toward the woman, he said to Simon, "Do you see this woman? I entered your house; you gave me no water for my feet, but she has bathed my feet with her tears and dried them with her hair. You gave me no kiss, but from the time I came in she has not stopped kissing my feet. You did not anoint my head with oil, but she has anointed my feet with ointment. Therefore, I tell you, her sins, which were many, have been forgiven; hence she has shown great love. But the one to whom little is forgiven, loves little." Then he said to her, "Your sins are forgiven." But those who were at the table with him began to say among themselves, "Who is this who even forgives sins?" and he said to the woman, "Your faith has saved you; go in peace" (Luke 7:36-50).

"What do you think? A man had two sons; he went to the first and said, 'Son, go and work in the vineyard today.' He answered, 'I will not'; but later he changed his mind and went. The father went to the second and said the same; and he answered, 'I go, sir'; but he did not go. Which of the two did the will of his father?" They said, "The first." Jesus said to them, "Truly I tell you, the tax collectors and the prostitutes are going into the kingdom of God ahead of you. For John came to you in the way of righteousness and you did not believe him, but the tax collectors and the prostitutes believed him; and even after you saw it, you did not change your minds and believe him" (Matthew 21:28-32).

Tax collectors, women with tainted reputations and Pharisees are the lead characters in the scriptural accounts. The tax collectors in Jesus' time make today's revenue assessors who play by the rules look benevolent. In New Testament times, the tax collectors' tactics were more like extortion. Not only were they collaborators with a foreign power to collect money to pay the Romans, they also had reputations for oppressing the poor for personal gain.

Illicit sexuality has always been an easy target for critics. The law of Moses not only forbade prostitution, but condoned stoning guilty parties (see Leviticus 19:29; Deuteronomy 22:21; John 8:2-11). The cultural climate made it easy to point fingers at what continues to be labelled "the world's oldest profession." In the time of Jesus, women were still considered acquisitions and often owned as property.

The Pharisees were part of the religious establishment of the day. Although they had minority membership in the courts of the Sanhedrin, their popularity with the people reinforced their religious authority. As keepers of both the written and oral law attributed to Moses, they pronounced and monitored what was religiously right. Their agenda was to defend the faith and entrench the Mosaic religious traditions. In their self-perceptions, they had no need for a spiritual doctor.

Jesus entered this cultural climate with another agenda. Rather than distancing himself from tax collectors, he recruited one of these prominent sinners to join his troupe. Instead of pointing an accusing finger at women with stained reputations, Jesus welcomed them into his presence. His mission-minded drive overruled his concern to protect his reputation. Jesus was a cultural boundary breaker. But it was his vision for the spiritually sick that motivated him to challenge the religious authorities and tangle with their views about what was religiously right.

Current Challenges

Guarding my reputation: In his "keep your distance—don't touch" world, Jesus allowed a woman to anoint his feet and use her hair for a towel. While confronting the religious establishment who denied their own sinfulness, he readily associated with sinners and commended their brand of spirituality. Jesus crossed lines that generated rumours that damaged his reputation. Most of us guard our reputations with a "safety first" strategy. What forces and factors keep us from taking more relational risks, living more adventurously or serving more creatively?

Human trafficking: These passages invite a focus on the current plight of sex workers and others in today's world who are subjected to human trafficking.

> *Trafficking in persons includes the recruitment, transportation, transfer, harbouring or receipt of persons, by means of the threat or use of force or other forms of coercion, of abduction, of fraud, of deception, of the abuse of power or of a position of vulnerability or of the giving or receiving of payments or benefits to achieve the consent of a person having control over another person, for the purpose of exploitation.* (Definition from United Nations Protocol, 2000)

Human trafficking is a flourishing modern-day form of slavery which The Salvation Army seeks to oppose across the world. Women and children are the most frequent sufferers of this injustice. Commercial exploitation is most often related to the sex industry, factory sweatshops, domestic servitude, agricultural labour and debt bondage.

Look back at Jesus in the above encounters. Assess his attitudes and actions. What can we learn from his example that can inform our own responses and practices to human trafficking?

For further information and suggestions for responding to human trafficking, check the International Social Justice Commission link on the international Salvation Army website: www.salvationarmy.org/isjc.

Prayers of Response

Close to home

Our God, over-indulgent drinking and the wrong kind of sex has been disastrous for so many people in so many places. We confess that even though there are impurities in our own hearts, we are still prone to judge other people's excesses. Our spirits reach out to those who are controlled by their uncontrolled indulgences. Prompt us always to believe in your invitation of grace to begin again. Teach us how to relate to people whose reputations are ruined. Show us how to be supportive to people whose lives are shattered. And forgive us when we falter ourselves. Amen.

Beyond our borders

Our Lord, we do not understand why there is so much pain in our world. Sometimes we feel that when we most need your presence that you are absent. We hear about soldiers who invade other countries and stop along the way to rape their prey. We know that living with the desperation of poverty forces young girls and boys into acts of prostitution. We cringe when we hear the stories of HIV-positive husbands and other men who intentionally inflict a death sentence on their victims. There is too much needless pain in our world. In your mercy, protect those who are so easily exploited. Amen.

Add your own specific prayers for those close to home and those beyond your borders.

The Salvation Army Story: Wading Into Hard Questions

He has told you, O mortal, what is good;
and what does the LORD require of you
but to do justice, and to love kindness,
and to walk humbly with your God?
(Micah 6:8)

The Bible asks questions that don't go away. Among the most persistent is Micah's question—"What does the LORD require of you?" It's a universal question to be asked of every human. But there is no *universal* human being. We are all creatures of particular times, places and cultures. Our particularity can't be ignored, and it shouldn't be.

The command to "act justly" is similarly universal. God demands it equally of every person. But justice means nothing when stripped of a context. When justice is the measure, culture is taken seriously. Sometimes culture is endorsed, sometimes rejected. Always it is taken into account. "How?" is the question.

~~~~

Gunpei Yamamuro was the first Japanese to become a commissioner in The Salvation Army. How he got to that point in a generation that reserved senior leadership almost exclusively for the British is an interesting story in itself. But it's questions earlier in his life that will be our focus.

Yamamuro had been an intellectually and morally serious youth, studying Confucian and Buddhist philosophy and aspiring to the Samurai virtues. When he became a Christian, he changed, of course, but he saw no need to reject everything he had aspired to before. " 'Bushido'... is the name given to the spirit which animated the Japanese fighting men of the old feudalistic era. This spirit evolved after many hundreds of years of strict discipline and training, and, as far as their light went, of moral rectitude, in the families of the warrior class. In this way a most virile and strong class of people came into existence.... If we of The Salvation Army ...

can assimilate the essence of this old-time spirit we shall be just the people to help Japan of today."

At the time of Yamamuro's conversion, however, most Japanese could not access Christianity. Not because there were no Christians in Japan (though Christian belief had been outlawed for 250 years prior to the Meiji restoration of 1868), but rather because Christian missionaries of the time targeted the upper-class and educated Japanese, and used a form of the Japanese language not understood by the masses. Romans 10:14 asks, "How are they to believe in one of whom they have never heard?" Yamamuro's analysis was that his fellow countrymen could not hear because of the way things were said more than by alien cultural values. Highfalutin language was a barrier to be challenged, for neither Yamamuro nor William Booth could be satisfied with a gospel only for the elites.

As a 16-year-old new to Christianity, Yamamuro had prayed, "O God, ... will you use and lead me to work for the salvation of the common people, to be a man who conveys the message of the gospel in a language to be understood by the uneducated, one who writes the truth in a way that anyone can read it and be enlightened?" As a 26-year-old, his prayer was answered when he wrote what was to become a landmark in vernacular Japanese literature. *Heimin no Fukuin* (Common People's Gospel) presented the message of Jesus in everyday language, weaving the history, cultural values and religious traditions of Japan together with the words of the Bible. So successful was the result that *Heimin no Fukuin* went through more than 500 printings and sold in excess of three million copies.

The Samurai virtues of loyalty, bravery and denial of self in the service of others could be baptized and refocused on Christ, but other values of Japanese culture could not be. During the Tokugawa shogunate (1603-1868), prostitution had been legalized and romanticized, even though there was seldom anything romantic about the real-life stories behind it. Entry into prostitution was typically a result of financial hardship—the daughters of poor, rural families being either sold to a brothel or held by the brothel as collateral on loans that kept the girls' families afloat. Prostituted women were confined to *yukaku* ("licensed quarters"), which were gated districts in the city comprising several brothels. The Yoshiwara (in English, "meadow of happiness") *yukaku* in Tokyo, for instance, was a mile square, walling in 5,000 prostituted women. Entry into and exit from the *yukaku* was carefully policed.

While it is true that the Meiji government overturned some of the laws of the Tokugawa era, outlawing slavery in 1872 and nullifying all debts where people were the collateral, little had actually changed. A woman might no longer be collateral on a debt, but to exit the brothel she still had to present the police with a "cessation" application requesting reclassification that had to be agreed to by the owner of her brothel and the head of her *yukaku* guild. Naturally, this rendered the supposedly liberating law moot.

Enraged by the injustice, Gunpei Yamamuro and other Salvationists devised a public campaign for "free cessation." The heart of the argument was that a woman should only have to present the police with a request signed by herself in order to leave the *yukaku*.

The campaign had several strategic prongs. One was to leave aside the question of prostitution per se, and focus on the exploitation and coerced confinement that most women in the *yukaku* experienced. A second was to provide human and material resources to shelter any women who wanted refuge. A third was publicity. Yamamuro's wife, Kiye, led the shelter work; Gunpei led communications.

A special "free cessation" issue of The Salvation Army's official publication, *Toki no Koe*, was commissioned. It was to be written colloquially and simply. Highborn or low, well-schooled or not, everyone was be able to get the point. "The gospel message was preceded by an extended treatment of the personal and social effects of prostitution. Yamamuro identified with the plight of these exploited women, apprising them of the 1872 law ... and informing them of The Salvation Army's desire to help in the process of social reintegration."

Salvationists distributed thousands of copies in Tokyo's five *yukaku*. Then, quite unplanned and unforeseen, major newspapers picked up the theme and reprinted Yamamuro's plea. Countering opposition from other publications (one titled, "The Immorality of Allowing Licensed Prostitutes to Stop their Business"), the mainstream press gave full coverage to the cause, promoting The Salvation Army's rescue work, and in the case of the daily newspaper *Niroku Shimpo*, turning the entire staff into on-the-ground campaigners for a day.

Yamamuro's special issue had come out August 1, 1900. By September 6, the Tokyo police changed their policy in order to facilitate free cessation, and by October 2, the national government made free cessation mandatory. In that one year, the number of licensed prostitutes in Tokyo dropped by 23 percent.[5]

~~~~

The commonalities with the "Maiden Tribute Campaign" in Bramwell Booth's England are evident. But the differences are equally important. Prostitution was not legal in England; it was in Japan. Cultured Englishmen would not admit to using prostitutes; there was no public shame attached to doing so in Japan. The government of Japan was keen to re-engage with western powers; England held the power to accept their overtures or not.

The point is that although the injustices done to Japanese women were as grievous as the injustices done to 19th-century English women or 21st-century women forced into the "sex trade" anywhere today, undoing injustice has no one-size-fits-all template. What must be asked is "What does the Lord require *here now*?"

We fail to do justice when we presume to be able to lift social injustice out of a particular context.

~~~~

When I was a cadet (and as I share this illustration, I can almost feel the guilt of shadow-land critics waving their index finger of condemnation at me), I participated in a War Cry *route with two other cadets on Saturday afternoons, as a good cadet should. We were placed in a high-rise area of low-rental apartments, so ministry was the more important goal than amassing collections for the moneybox.*

The three of us found ourselves one Saturday afternoon, after a rap on a certain door, invited in by a shout from behind the door.

"Open the door, I can't get up."

I put my hand on the door handle and the voice now appeared as a man so shrivelled that his armchair almost hid him from view. Entering, we sat down and chatted about a number of things. He shared with us about his medical condition, which basically told us we were looking at a man dying of alcoholism. Just before we were to leave he had one request.

"Could you light me a cigarette?"

"Well, I suppose we could strike a match."

But even that was not possible.

"I've run out of matches," he said. "Just light it from the stove—you can see it's difficult for me to get up."

Well, silence crammed the space in the room. The three of us looked at each other, our pristine uniforms proclaiming The Salvation Army's official stand.

He said again, "Oh come on, what's wrong with you?"

Rising from my chair, I became what some might call a culprit, and some might call a saviour. What does the Lord require?

"Give me your cigarette," I said, and to the stove I went.

Cigarette in mouth, and bending into the stove burner, I lit it. Believe me, I did not inhale! But that man acted as if I had brought him a gift from heaven.

The next week he was no longer there and word came that he had died just a few days after our visit.

Years later, during my tenure as the leader of The Salvation Army in Papua New Guinea, I found that I still was not always ready for what met me.

Picture a Salvation Army proclamation of the gospel on a Sunday afternoon in a market setting of fresh vegetables and fruit. Sales did not bring in enough for the vendors to feel comfortable. We were singing, "What a friend we have in Jesus." Powerful harmonies. Two little girls were sitting cross-legged in front of our band of good news. My eye was drawn to them. How considerate, I thought, that the older sister was a wall for the younger to lean back on. As the older rummaged through the hair of her little sister, I thought "how affectionate." Then I discovered I was missing the real action as fingers in hair were actually retrieving the catch of the day. The catch was squeezed in the fingers of the stronger and popped into the mouths of the hungry. Nits were the food and I was being confronted with a cultural nuance that made the insides of this white woman ex-pat reel with anger, horror and the question: "What does the Lord require of me?"—MCM

~~~~

Micah lived some time between 750 and 696 BC. He saw what was wrong in the culture in which he lived. He saw how social sin impacted the small towns and villages of his country of Judah. He saw how the rich treated the poor. It wasn't right. He saw the poor lose their homes and their land. It wasn't right. He saw a lack of kindness, a lack of justice, a lack of humility. He saw religious leaders, business people and other people in authority use their power in evil ways. Micah called out and said what was wrong in that time, at that place.

He teaches us that God expects justice of people. But he also teaches us that social justice shaped by Micah 6:8 measures faithfulness with *questions*. Real justice probes, mercy embraces, humility acts—with the immeasurable God in view.

Human beings like *solutions*. We'd like to think of injustice as a "problem" and of ourselves as smart enough to problem-solve, tie a pretty bow around a policy framework and a strategic rollout plan, and present it all back to God, mission accomplished. In reality, however, a triune partnership of justice, mercy and humility is a balancing act that defies the tidy approaches of organizational management.

~~~~

I recall sitting in the boardroom of a well-heeled foundation with donors of exceptional wealth. The dream was to inoculate every child in the world under five and thereby eliminate deadly diseases so that five-year-olds could turn six. What could be wrong with that? My imagination flew to continents where the little ones whose arms were being discussed lived. Those at the table were not the ones rolling up their sleeves for some needle. I spoke up with this image in mind and voiced my thoughts: "What if an inoculated child dies of hunger the next day?"

Our approach to injustice could appear to be noble and life-giving and permit us to pat ourselves on the back, but injustice is wily. It finds victims in all sorts of ways. I wonder if a culture of abundance dreams up ideas that are as thin as the paper they are written on.

This is not to point the finger at well-meaning organizations. How many times do I myself ask the question: "What does the Lord require of me?" It's an easy ask in worshipful settings of music, preachment and comfortable pews. Perhaps that's not the best place to hear God's question, though. Perhaps God wants to put the question to us while we are facing the chaotic conditions that others are forced to endure. We are all born into what is known as family, ethnicity, geography and culture. Some of us are very comfortable. We belong. Most often we feel safe. For us, life is lived with more answers than questions. Then social media flashes us images that strike out at our comfort with discomfort. Injustice cannot be contained. It bleeds across nations, rivers of evil winding the way of oppression, crushing opportunities for far too many. Hearing the question "What does the Lord require?" could just start us off in getting our feet wet, wading into the waters of injustice with more questions than answers.—MCM

When justice is the measure—hard questions are not ducked.

What is the right program strategy for the present—and the future?
What is the right international resource allocation?
What is the right mission scope?
What is the right balance for global decision making?
What is the right emphasis that affirms both corps ministries and social services?

Which of the old ways should pass away?

What new ways should replace what is on life support?

When Isaiah 61:8 says, "I the LORD love justice," the Creator is revealing a principle. We, the creation and the people of God, are to echo God. If God loves justice and hates wrongdoing, so should we.

But it is not only a *principle* that God is revealing. The God who loves justice acts to *create* justice. We are to discover an approach to justice that re-echoes our trust in God to lead us. For us as The Salvation Army, trust in God has always been both personal and interpersonal. Justice is an act of faith with expectant hopefulness. It takes us beyond thinking about God dwelling in the perfection of heaven into the world that God so loves. Entering the world's wastelands with pathways that are longing to be made straight, we enter with the God who loves justice.

CHAPTER 3

CONFRONTING THE POWERFUL

Shout out, do not hold back! (Isaiah 58:1)

This is no time to speak softly.
The risks are too high,
The people of Israel are on a dark path,
Their postures are pious but their deeds are evil.

The prophet Isaiah blows his trumpet—
  "God's people are pretenders,
  They fast in public to feel good in private,
  They parade virtue but practise vice,
  Their form of godliness is drowned in their hypocrisy."

Then—the prophet takes a deep breath and changes his tone—
  "There is still time to worship and pray and be still,
  But true godliness breaks out of the prison of self-interest.
  Fasting is converted into feeding the hungry,
  Prayers are translated into shelter out of the cold,
  Worship inspires the work of lightening the load of the poor,
  The oppressed are given keys to unlock their restraints."

The light of justice breaks into the dawn of a new day.
And the God who waits for hypocrisy to subside and injustice to
be defeated whispers, "Here I am"
[Isaiah 58:1-9a, paraphrase].

A s we transition into the second half of this book, a candid focus
on the human costs and consequences of injustice is in order.
We are challenged by the reality that injustice has both
individual and social dimensions. We know that personal injustice is
often the consequence of structural injustice. We are reminded that—

WHEN: Eight-year-olds cannot read; families cannot drink water without getting sick; HIV-positive women cannot protect their newborn babies; funerals displace preventable deaths;

WHEN: Children go to bed hungry seven nights a week; parents bury their children because they died of malaria; women, young girls and boys are exploited as sex slaves; workers labour for scandalous wages to fashion designer clothes;

WHEN: The earth is abused without regard for future generations; skin colour and social status padlock doors of opportunity; the healthy and educated cannot use their strengths to work;

WHEN: The righteous and holy disregard the impoverished and unclean; God's compassion is closeted in sanctuaries and temples; the strong and the privileged disregard the weak and the oppressed;

THEN: Injustice rules; countless lives are squandered; our shared humanity is disgraced and darkness prevails.

As followers of Jesus, our vision for a more just world is dependent on two primary "delivery systems," social and spiritual.

Social-Order Justice: Social order is a mark of a healthy society—and a healthy society commits to the well-being of all its citizens. It is social order, including citizen rights and responsibilities, that makes the prospect of a just society a possibility. In civil societies, the pursuit of justice is a priority mandate of public policy.

As previously noted, a just social order embeds *ethical/human-rights justice* in a culture. Acknowledging the differing capacities between more-developed and less-developed countries, the goal is equitable access for all peoples to the benefits of the nation. Among their other responsibilities, politicians exist to ensure the right of access to education, health care and necessities such as safe water.

Strategies to ensure an economy that can support the livelihood of families are an essential priority. Banks keep money in circulation. Lending practices are reliable. Interest rates are fair. Political corruption is not tolerated. Although businesses may be profit-motivated, their social contribution is to provide services and products that generate jobs. Creating space for entrepreneurial innovation that challenges the status quo is the norm. Competition generates high performance.

When proper societal structures are in place, the resulting social order delivers strong measures of justice for all. Making space for ethnic diversity and other expressions of difference will protect minority communities. Allocating resources so the unemployed can pursue vocational retraining, sheltering the disabled and publicly funding welfare programs all contribute to the justice vision.

When seeking to build a healthy society, whether individuals are productive givers or primary receivers, there are no reasons to compromise a commitment to a high work ethic. Some people will need extra assistance for a time, and there will be exceptions; however, the goal will always be economic sustainability and social dignity for all.

Spiritual-Transformation Justice: When God's people get it right, they bring a distinctive contribution to the justice table. Even though followers of Jesus do not have sole access to human virtue or an exclusive claim on being principled people, they have two advantages: Christians have Scripture to help them discern God's will and ways for themselves and others; and they have the historical Jesus who demonstrated the best of what human life can and should be.

Have no illusions, followers of Jesus will never duplicate the full beauty and wisdom of the Christ of history. But their faith points them in the right direction. The understanding they gain from Scripture and their relationship with God's Spirit can enable them to translate their convictions into compassionate behaviour that serves the interests of others.

Accordingly, Christians who have integrated world views will compute what is going on around them with the mind of Christ. Government budgets will be viewed as moral documents. Spending priorities will be scrutinized with informed moral reasoning.

Instead of automatically resisting tax increases, resource allocations will be assessed for their priorities of social-need spending. Corporations will be expected to carry their fair share of the tax burden responsibility. Those with more wealth will acknowledge that it is the strength of society that has helped make their wealth possible and they will be challenged to share with those who have less. Churches will speak collectively into the public forum and mobilize the voices of their people.

The call for social-order justice and adequate taxation to respond to social-need spending should not be confused with the development of a welfare state. The state should not be expected to simply cater to the wishes of her citizens. Neither should dysfunctional families assume they can simply turn to the state to cure their ills. Mutual responsibility—the state doing its part and individuals and families doing their part—is a necessary balance.

Particular circumstances will influence the responses that God's people express. But the patterns will be predictable. They will embrace a world that is bigger than their own. Self-interest or material gain will not have the final word. God's people will champion the marginalized and be driven by the ethic of love. Right relationships will rule the day. Neighbour love will prevail.

Justice will trump injustice—every time. And quietly, the people of God who live this way will know that the God who has forgiven and restored them has made them better people than they would ever have been on their own. And regardless of their beliefs, power brokers who have a vision for the potential of social-order justice will welcome the participation of people of faith as allies in the pursuit of life as it is meant to be lived.

Challenging Unjust Behaviour

In Jesus' time and in ours, seeking justice is a struggle. We are often forced to resign ourselves to the reality that some justice is better than no justice. We console ourselves with the fact that more justice is better than less justice. But we hang on with hope, believing that full justice is attainable. Only then will we be able to celebrate with others as they experience sustainable justice.

Encountering God in the Biblical Story

Speak to yourself like no one else is listening;
Listen to others like no one else is listening.

- Read the story in unison as a group.
- In silence, reflect on your first impressions.
- Continue in silence. This time read the story looking carefully at Zacchaeus' behaviour.
- Write down what captures your attention about Zacchaeus.
- Continuing in silence, read the story a third time, looking carefully at the behaviour of Jesus.
- Write down what captures your attention about Jesus.
- Share your written insights with each other.

Jesus entered Jericho and was passing through it. A man was there named Zacchaeus; he was a chief tax collector and was rich. He was trying to see who Jesus was, but on account of the crowd he could not, because he was short in stature. So he ran ahead and climbed a sycamore tree to see him, because he was going to pass that way. When Jesus came to the place, he looked up and said to him, "Zacchaeus, hurry and come down; for I must stay at your house today." So he hurried down and was happy to welcome him. All who saw it began to grumble and said, "He has gone to be the guest of one who is a sinner." Zacchaeus stood there and said to the Lord, "Look, half of my possessions, Lord, I will give to the poor; and if I have defrauded anyone of anything, I will pay back four times as much." Then Jesus said to him, "Today salvation has come to this house, because he too is a son of

Abraham. For the Son of Man came to seek out and to save the lost"
(Luke 19:1-10).

The encounter Jesus had with Zacchaeus was not a crafted parable. This real-life exchange was with a walking, thinking, feeling, innovative, but conniving, individual. As a tax collector, Zacchaeus was part of the Roman revenue machine that should have been contributing to social order and justice for all.

The Jewish cultural consensus was clear. Tax collectors were sinners. They were scoundrels on a number of counts. Working for the Romans was considered collaboration with the enemy. This perception was reinforced by the Roman practice of selling tax collecting franchises to the highest bidder. Tax collectors could use whatever tactics necessary to extract all they could from the populace so long as they paid their quota to the Roman authorities.

Spiritually speaking, tax collectors were judged as people who sold themselves to a life of sin and deliberate disregard for God's ways.

Zacchaeus was rich at the expense of others and socially marginalized. He was considered the chief of sinners. Given the circumstances, Jesus was criticized for his lack of judgment. Here he was having a lavish meal with a rich sinner.

Current Challenges

Sharing a meal in someone else's home can be revealing. There is a sense that you do not really know someone until you have spent time with them in their home. Their style of hospitality—pictures of their family, art on the walls, an ambiance of contentment or tension—all speak to people's private reality. Their personal space reveals an aspect of their true selves not on display in their workplace. Imagine what Zacchaeus' home was like. Project yourself into the conversation Zacchaeus and Jesus had around the table. How would you describe the tone of their talk? The results indicate that at some point Jesus challenged Zacchaeus' practices. What do you think was the focus of their interaction?

The encounter between Zacchaeus and Jesus generated two primary outcomes: one was social and the other was spiritual. Zacchaeus reordered his public behaviour. He became compassionate toward the poor and started sharing his riches. He admitted his coercive tactics and committed to generous restitution. Spiritually, Zacchaeus experienced forgiveness and salvation. The mission of Jesus to seek and rescue the spiritually lost was fulfilled in two essential ways. Zacchaeus restored his relationship with the God who loved him and the people he cheated experienced just treatment. Think about the impact on the people who lived in Jericho. What rumours must have circulated in the community? What did people start saying about both Zacchaeus and Jesus?

Think about your own community: neighbours, friends, church associates, work colleagues. What rumours would you like them to hear about you? If you could receive a "faith compliment" from your friends or work colleagues, what would you like to hear them say? What would you like people in the community to say about your church?

Even the thought of paying taxes can fill a sunny day with clouds. At tax time, feeling the tension between the legal right of tax avoidance and the illegal temptation of tax evasion is common. But in most societies, taxation is what makes social order possible. Focus on your own community. If you had control over political policy in your community, which two or three social sectors would receive priority tax resources?

Prayers of Response

Close to home

Our God, thank you for reminding us that people of faith are people with a conscience. Zacchaeus' experience challenges us. We are mindful that the journey from unbelief to belief calls for profound changes. Personal salvation is more than a private encounter. Faith invades the public space of our vocations. We accept the inevitable scrutiny of our ethics, our morals and our conduct. We need your help to live with integrity. Along the way, sensitize us to open our ears to the whispers of your spirit. Amen.

Beyond our borders
Our living God, Jesus challenged Zacchaeus about his personal sin and his professional practices. He acted. "Salvation came to his house" and restitution brought justice to those he had cheated. We pray that in situations where people have been exploited that the exploiters would have the courage to make matters right. We also lift up cultures and countries where people are not allowed to examine their beliefs and change their religious convictions. Because you have invited us to "choose this day whom we will serve," we pray that religious freedom will be granted to people everywhere. Amen.

Add your own specific prayers for those close to home and those beyond your borders.

Confronting the Spiritually Arrogant

The ultimate expression of spiritual arrogance is self-righteousness. The self-righteous are the "good" people. They have only one point of view. They hear with one ear and see with one eye. They are more inclined to pronounce than to listen. The closed systems they live in predispose them to judge others. And they are ready to impose their will and ways whether others agree with them or not.

It would be a mistake to limit self-righteousness to the realm of religion. Advocates for the environment, personal-prerogative-sexuality, anti-smoking, pro-life and anti-abortion can all exhibit the same one-sided clamour for their cause. That doesn't mean the self-righteous do not have virtues to admire. They can be counted on to stand up for their convictions, and often their intentions are honourable. Still, if you hold different views and are the recipient of their judgment, the self-righteous are tough to love.

Encountering God in the Biblical Story

> *Acknowledge where you are indifferent and cast it aside,*
> *Discern where your spirit is quiet when it should be*
> *disturbed,*
> *Create space for passion to reside in your soul.*

- Read the section on Sabbath standards silently.
- Read the passage again silently, with a focus on the Pharisees.
- Write down your observations about the Pharisees.
- Read the passage a third time silently, with a focus on Jesus.
- Write down your observations on the actions of Jesus.
- Share your observations, contrasting the Pharisees and Jesus.
- Now read aloud the section on hypocrisy denounced.
- Take a few moments to project yourself into the crowd. Prepare to listen to Jesus' outburst as a member of the crowd or as one of the disciples.
- Read the text again out loud. What is the strongest message you hear?

- If you are working with a group, share your message with the others.

One Sabbath while Jesus was going through the grain fields, his disciples plucked some heads of grain, rubbed them in their hands, and ate them. But some of the Pharisees said, "Why are you doing what is not lawful on the Sabbath?" Jesus answered, "Have you not read what David did when he and his companions were hungry? He entered the house of God and took and ate the bread of the Presence, which it is not lawful for any but the priests to eat, and gave some to his companions?" Then he said to them, "The Son of Man is lord of the Sabbath."

On another Sabbath he entered the synagogue and taught, and there was a man there whose right hand was withered. The scribes and the Pharisees watched him to see whether he would cure on the Sabbath, so that they might find an accusation against him. Even though he knew what they were thinking, he said to the man who had the withered hand, "Come and stand here." He got up and stood there. Then Jesus said to them, "I ask you, is it lawful to do good or to do harm on the Sabbath, to save life or to destroy it?" After looking around at all of them, he said to him, "Stretch out your hand." He did so, and his hand was restored. But they were filled with fury and discussed with one another what they might do to Jesus (Luke 6:1-11).

Then Jesus said to the crowds and to his disciples, "The scribes and the Pharisees sit on Moses' seat; therefore, do whatever they teach you and follow it; but do not do as they do, for they do not practise what they teach.

"Woe to you, scribes and Pharisees, hypocrites! For you tithe mint, dill and cumin, and have neglected the weightier matters of the law: justice and mercy and faith. It is these you ought to have practised without neglecting the others. You blind guides! You strain out a gnat but swallow a camel!

"Woe to you, scribes and Pharisees, hypocrites! For you clean the outside of the cup and of the plate, but inside they are full of greed and self-indulgence. You blind Pharisee! First clean the inside of the cup, so that the outside also may become clean.

"Woe to you, scribes and Pharisees, hypocrites! For you are like

whitewashed tombs, which on the outside look beautiful, but inside they are full of the bones of the dead and of all kinds of filth. So you also on the outside look righteous to others, but inside you are full of hypocrisy and lawlessness" (Matthew 23:1-3, 23-28).

Jesus' agenda put him at odds with the self-righteousness of the religious elite. The Pharisees and the scribes were the religious power people of the day. They had social standing and spiritual authority. The Pharisees were a small but influential group who upheld the standards of the law and ritual purity. They were scholars who were well-informed and respected by the people. The scribes were also part of the religious establishment. They dominated the hierarchy of the priests who supervised the temple worship. Together with the priests, scribes and Pharisees comprised the Sanhedrin, which functioned as the Jewish court system. Accordingly, they were not just public teachers and interpreters of the religious law, they also served as judges to enforce the laws of the state.

In that Mosaic tradition, the scribes and Pharisees had both political power and religious stature. Jesus' progressive teaching, his open critique of their brand of righteousness and his increasing popularity with the people put him on a crash course with the existing power structure (see Matthew 5:20). Jesus refused to bless their restrictive application of Mosaic law and their pervasive control over the Israelites. Compared to Jesus' example of how to love God and serve your neighbour, the legalism of the scribes and Pharisees amounted to religious oppression. And oppression was what Jesus lived to liberate.

Current Challenges

Religion that majors on minors is oppressive. When faith is choked by legalism instead of being the aroma of life, it smells and tastes like death. According to Jesus, some religious matters—such as justice, mercy and faith—are more important than others. What checks and balances can we put in place to keep us focused on spiritual priorities and protect us from diversions into spiritual wastelands?

In your world, whom do you associate with religious power? Where should we look for our sources of religious authority? How can we protect ourselves from the abuses of misguided religious power? Who has the responsibility to keep religious leaders accountable?

The pretence of godliness is another route to religious oppression. And while we all need measures of grace and mercy, unless we attempt to live the life of faith, we are imposters. Reflect back on your journey of faith. Identify times when how you lived your faith energized you and when you felt liberated to live as God created you to live. If you are working with a group, share a story to illustrate.

Prayers of Response

Close to home
O Lord, we are attracted to certainty. We feel more secure when we are clear about what is right and what is wrong. Still, we know there are errors in our minds. We can't get it all right. We understand that your faith family is much larger than The Salvation Army or our particular church. Don't let us be satisfied with private piety. Free us from petty orthodoxy. Keep us from dying on senseless crosses. Help us discern the essentials of faith from the many expressions of faith. Keep us from being judgmental of others when they should be sensing our acceptance. Show us how to be true to ourselves and respectful of others. Amen.

Beyond our borders
Creator God, there is a dark side of religion. Too many people have died when they have been on the wrong side of the religious power in their land. Children have been abused. Women have been demeaned. Families have been alienated from each other. Instead of being an instrument of peace, faith has been a dagger of death. Lord, have mercy. In these times, we acknowledge the tensions between Muslims and Christians. You have created our planet to be large enough for the co-existence of different faiths. Grant us wisdom to know how to create space for "the other." Teach us how to deal with our differences and live together graciously. Amen.

Add your own specific prayers for those close to home and those beyond your borders.

Reordering Political Power

The interface between politics and religion has a long history. In many instances, the mix has been explosive. In Old Testament times, the Jewish people were ruled by the laws of the Torah. The commandments to love the Lord your God and your neighbour as yourself were part of Scripture, but considered inadequate to inform all the dilemmas involved in living a godly life. As a theocracy, the Mosaic religious law was the societal standard.

No political system is perfect. Many Islamic republics institute religious repression. Some monarchies and dictatorships are intolerant of religious diversity. Marxism and communism remove social space for God and replace it with atheism. Even democratic societies are pressed with the evolving will of the people and their perpetually changing beliefs and preferred behaviours.

Encountering God in the Biblical Story

> Read for information,
> Meditate for understanding,
> Contemplate for restoration,
> Implement for faithful living.

- Read the two passages below, consecutively and out loud.
- Read the Mark passage about paying taxes out loud again, this time putting yourself in Jesus' position. How do you think you would have felt? What might you have said?
- Now transition back to the Matthew passage and read it out loud. Listen carefully. Jesus makes a number of distinct statements. Identify a single statement that captures your attention. If you are working with a group, share your observation and comment on why it is significant to you.

Then they sent to him some Pharisees and some Herodians to trap him in what he said. And they came and said to him, "Teacher, we know that you are sincere, and show deference to no one; for you do not regard people with partiality, but teach the way of God in accordance with truth. *Is it lawful to pay taxes to the emperor, or not? Should we pay them, or should we not?" But knowing their hypocrisy, he said to them, "Why are you putting me to the test? Bring me a denarius and let me see it." And they brought one. Then he said to them, "Whose head is this, and whose title?" They answered, "The emperor's." Jesus said to them, "Give to the emperor the things that are the emperor's, and to God the things that are God's." And they were utterly amazed at him* (Mark 12:13-17).

Then the mother of the sons of Zebedee came to him with her sons, and kneeling before him, she asked a favour of him. And he said to her, "What do you want?" She said to him, "Declare that these two sons of mine will sit, one at your right hand and one at your left, in your kingdom." But Jesus answered, "You do not know what you are asking. Are you able to drink the cup that I am about to drink?" They said to him, "We are able." He said to them, "You will indeed drink my cup, but to sit at my right hand and at my left, this is not mine to grant, but it is for those for whom it has been prepared by my Father."

When the 10 heard it, they were angry with the two brothers. But Jesus called them to him and said, "You know that the rulers of the Gentiles lord it over them, and their great ones are tyrants over them. It will not be so among you; but whoever wishes to be great among you must be your servant, and whoever wishes to be first among you must be your slave; just as the Son of Man came not to be served but to serve, and to give his life a ransom for many" (Matthew 20:20-28).

Political and religious tensions surrounded Jesus in his day. In the predicament conveyed in Mark 12, Jesus was being monitored with the intent to entrap him into transgressing either civil law or religious law. The Pharisees were looking for a reason to accuse him. So were the Herodians, representatives of King Herod who controlled the secular state of Galilee on behalf of Rome. Despite their differences, the two groups were ready to collaborate if it meant finding fault with Jesus. With veiled motives, they employed pretence and flattery in an attempt to trick Jesus.

The encounter recorded in Matthew 20 launches us into the dilemma of how political leaders should use their power and authority. The situation reveals how confused the disciples were about the nature of the "kingdom" that Jesus was establishing. James and John were thinking about their future positions in a new government order. Rather than making a personal appeal to be the next prime minister and director of finance, they hid behind their mother who made the request to Jesus on their behalf. The other disciples were not impressed. They began squabbling among themselves. Jesus had heard enough. He gathered his disciples around him for a teachable moment. His tone was stern. The implications were startling. His directive was decisive: *"It will not be so among you."*

Current Challenges

The brilliant response Jesus gave to his adversaries indicated that his followers must fulfil their obligations to both God and the state: "Give to the emperor the things that are the emperor's, and to God the things that are God's." The directive invites dual citizenship: be a citizen of the kingdom of God and a citizen of your country. Identify areas of life where God's laws and government laws reinforce each other. Where can the two conflict?

A primary role of government is to provide equitable services and keep social order. Identify a social segment of the population that has specific needs but has been left out of the political planning in your community/city. Suggest recommendations that would address the vulnerabilities of those who are ignored.

Jesus critiques the methods and priorities of the governing rulers in his day: "You know that the rulers of the Gentiles lord it over them, and their great ones are tyrants over them. It will not be so among you; but whoever wishes to be great among you must be your servant." The message is clear: political power is to be used to serve. Rather than seeking personal gain, politicians are to use their authority over people to serve the best interests of the people in their constituencies. What mechanisms are in place where you live, and what additional systems are needed to keep politicians accountable?

God's aspiration for equity and justice transcends all political ideologies. The responsibility to seek justice is not the domain of any race or creed. Neither is the practice of pursuing justice the exclusive right of any nation or culture. Create a list of countries that currently have reputations for ignoring human rights. Identify their systems of government. Identify their leaders by name. Create and share a prayer list that invites people to become aware and intercede. Keep open to ideas that call for intervention.

Prayers of Response

Close to home

Gracious God, we believe that good governance is part of your design for creation. We pay our taxes with a vision that our collective resources will contribute to a more just society. Our hope is that our political decision makers will live with a concern for the common good. We live with desires that all our citizens will have equity of access to our cultural advantages and social benefits. We also know that the combination of power, authority and money can be lethal. And we often struggle with our vision for the reign of God and the priorities of the political party in power. Give us the insight of faith that equips us to think with the mind of Christ and grant us wisdom to discern when to speak out and when to be silent. Amen.

Beyond our borders

Creator God, we pray for our elected political leaders and government decision makers. We thank you for them. We choose to believe they want to serve with good intentions. We acknowledge they deal with complexities that we know not of. We can imagine the web of temptations that weave their way into their lives. Grant them strength to live with integrity. Protect them from being strangled by thorns of corruption. Give them an awareness of the virtue and vulnerability of their power—their capacity for both good and evil. We lift them up to you and your guidance. Amen.

Add your own specific prayers for those close to home and those beyond your borders.

The Salvation Army Story: Spending Our Collateral

"Shout out, do not hold back!"
(Isaiah 58:1)

Isaiah 58 was one of William Booth's favourite texts. We are pressed to wonder why? And if he was challenged by its prophetic words, should we be troubled in the same way?

The predicaments in Isaiah 58 give us insight. The city walls are so damaged that families cannot be safe. There are big potholes in the streets that everyone counts on for commerce. People with money power are guilty of unspeakable evil. And their celebrity status lets them get away with it.

We are pressed to wonder if power is always corrupt. Can it be redeemed? What does it take for social influence to be put to good purpose?

The realism of the Bible tells us that sin has infected every part of creation. But the Bible also tells us that the power structures of the world are no more or less fallen than individual human beings. Colossians confirms that God created power structures as well as individual people: "Thrones, dominions, rulers or powers—all things have been created through him and for him" (Colossians 1:16).

Power structures are means to good ends when obedience to God's intentions are in charge. They make it possible for human beings to flourish. And even when they have gone astray, God's interventions can redeem them in Christ. However, if the poor are going to be protected and empowered, we will need to be a part of God's interventions. Our partnership with God and the poor will demand a willingness to challenge power structures and policy inequities.

Speaking gospel truth to power people will require a different set of skills than speaking the truth of the gospel to individuals. And here is where William Booth excelled. The social analysis articulated in *In Darkest England and the Way Out*[6] reveals a distinctive kind of intelligence. In order for us to assess and engage in critical social analysis in our time, we will need Christian mind savvy and bold resolve.

~~~~

During my appointment time in London, England, The Salvation Army had undertaken a major study on homelessness. We began to rebuild old dormitory hostels with a view to introducing a philosophy of investing in others through their capacity to change. The day came when the Westminster Hostel, a stone's throw from Westminster Abbey, had drawn up architectural plans for a major rebuild. This meant resettlement for residents who had lived many years in their cots covered with bedspreads imprinted with the Salvation Army shield.

I set up an interview team to pose questions to the residents who were getting nervous about their future. The first question focused on their dreams. The responses were informative and diverse. Some said, "I've been waiting 10 years for someone to ask my opinion." Others said, "I want my own place." What was first dismissively labelled as just hostel men speaking up became a challenge to us to consider their seemingly high expectations.

While this process was going on, I discovered that the territory was about to sell off a tourist hotel. The "For Sale" sign was going up. At the time, I was far from being a commissioner and reticent to speak out. However, I decided to make an appointment with the chief secretary. I reasoned: "We need a place for the men who are about to be displaced from the Westminster Hostel. Can we have the hotel? We will pay rent."

The chief secretary was open enough to bring the suggestion to the administration. To no one's surprise, resistance began to surface. "They'll wreck the place." "What will the upscale neighbours think?" But in this situation, compassion and persistence won the day.

I arrived early on the moving day at the Westminster Hostel. Other team members were also there, along with the public relations officer with his camera and notepad. The men at the hostel, clasping their plastic bags, climbed into the vans and off they went. I stood in the hostel courtyard where thousands of men had come for over a hundred years, then realized the hotel was their next stop. I wondered: "How will it go?" Suddenly I felt a pang of dread: "Are we creating a disaster? Is this just a crazy idea?" Had I thrown away the keys of successful institutionalization and sold all the credibility we had built up over decades?

Arriving at the tourist hotel will always remain as a treasured memory. Stepping into the carpeted and chandeliered foyer, I began to feel as if I was in a magical, twinkling Never-Never Land. I hardly recognized the men. Their demeanour was like a dance in slow motion as they were each given their own space with amenities that they had only shared with strangers in the past.

I recall one man with red hair and beard who had never smiled. That day his beard took on a different shape because of the grin beneath. His eyes shone with hope. I was trancelike as I took in a miracle that was like celebrating feeding the 5,000 or changing water into wine. The "least of these" had new power. They walked taller. They were given new opportunities to be responsible. They tasted human dignity— maybe for the first time in their lives.

I walked out of the transformed tourist hotel thinking about how fearful I had been to challenge the Salvation Army decision makers. I thought about the power dynamics when people move from dependence to measures of independence. I heard the words of Isaiah 58:8: "If you do these things, your salvation will come like the dawn" (NLT).—MCM

~~~~

In a later time, on a different continent, in another social context, comparable impacts are being achieved through the Ray and Joan Kroc Corps Community Centers in the United States.

Ray had been the founder of McDonald's, of "golden arches" fame. When his widow, Joan, gifted $1.8 billion to The Salvation Army in 2003, more than one person mused that it would prove to be the tail that wagged the dog. They feared that The Salvation Army would be co-opted by the money and that mission-drift would engulf us. While the experiment is still in its early days and not every initiative will be equally successful, there certainly is reason to think the fears were exaggerated. The intent of the money is being actualized. The justice vision is being realized.

Joan Kroc's wish was that The Salvation Army would have the money to build state-of-the-art facilities in communities that in some ways were "blighted." That's a tough word, but it describes a tough reality. In the United States today, *some* children have all they need. They have strong families, churches, schools, athletic facilities, art galleries, skilled coaches, teachers and spiritual guides that give them every opportunity to flourish. In contrast, many other children live without. They experience impoverished conditions.

A blighted community lacks the tax base to sustain quality education. Crime increases. More people move out than move in. This, in turn, shrinks the tax base further and makes local business unprofitable. The creation of a just society is virtually impossible.

Good jobs have the opposite effects. Employed workers buy groceries, employ babysitters and go to shows. They pay taxes that provide for schools, roads, police and clean water. The common good is served.

The general economic downturn that affected the whole country after 2008 had hit some places especially hard. South Bend, Indiana, was such a place. The Salvation Army made a deliberate decision to continue its plans for a Kroc Center, knowing it may be among the few construction projects moving forward at the time.

Brandon, a self-employed professional electrician, was hired as part of The Salvation Army's commitment to award a percentage of the contracts to minority-owned local businesses. At the opening, Brandon gave his testimony beaming with pride at what his efforts had helped build. A general contractor who also had a role in building the Kroc Center heard him, knew the quality of his work and offered Brandon more work.

While structural injustice may have fed personal greed and created the global economic crisis, stories like Brandon's show that if organizations such as The Salvation Army who have money or political clout open the door of opportunity for others, they can pave the way toward social justice.

~~~~

The Salvation Army has not always been convicted about using its resources in the cause of justice, however. General Shaw Clifton's study of Salvation Army attitudes toward war from the Crimean War through the Second World War demonstrates that The Salvation Army was generally mute and pragmatically self-protective.[7] General Clifton concludes that sometimes we were co-opted by others' political ideology. Troublingly, we did not invest the resources needed to form and voice our own principled Christian positions. Other parts of the church spoke out against the evils of the day. We did not. It's a part of our history that we tend to keep in low light.

~~~~

By contrast, the Maiden Tribute Campaign is probably the best-known story of The Salvation Army taking up the social justice cause. We can't retell the details here. Others have done that, in any case. Read Frederick Coutts' *Bread for my Neighbour*, for instance. But we can draw attention to the fact it is a true story of unknown people, such as Rebecca Jarrett and Madame Combe, partnering with more influential people, such as Josephine Butler, Bramwell Booth and W.T. Stead. Their shared cause was to change laws that had failed to protect young women from sexual exploitation and abuse. At the time, The Salvation Army did not have the public collateral that it has today. Still, it used what it had to amplify the influence of a media celebrity—W.T. Stead—and mobilize a grassroots movement of 300,000 citizens to petition Parliament. The political powers listened. The law was changed.

Historians tell us that Catherine and William Booth were actually ambivalent about the whole episode—their Salvation Army has always been wary of political engagement. But history has also proved that it was a right thing to do. The Salvation Army dared to confront the powerful for the sake of the powerless. And justice was served.

"It made us known," Bramwell Booth wrote, "and put us at one stroke in the very front rank of those who were contending for the better treatment of the lost and the poor; and while it roused some powerful enemies, especially in the press, the enmity lasted only for a time."[8]

~~~~

The Social Policy and Parliamentary Unit (SPPU) in New Zealand[9] continues today with the same spirit that inspired the Maiden Tribute Campaign.

When a 2003 survey revealed that The Salvation Army had failed to arrest a decline in the social circumstances of New Zealand's most vulnerable groups, Salvation Army leadership created a specialist unit focused on engaging with social policy and social justice.

The SPPU was intentionally housed in an Auckland neighbourhood of high need. The purpose was to keep research and policy staff within a busy social service centre and engaged with the community. The initial research project, "A New Zealand that Demands Attention," created immediate response from politicians, the media and the unit's target group of influential leaders.

In ensuing years, evidence-based research has centred on justice reform, forgotten people, alcohol abuse, consumerism, human trafficking, youth and children's policy and housing issues. Housing reports have covered state rental housing practices and policies to create home ownership. Annually, a State of the Nation report assesses five areas of social policy: New Zealand's children, work and incomes, housing, crime and punishment, and social hazards.

Recommendations advocated by the SPPU have frequently been incorporated into government policy. SPPU staff have been part of public policy groups, government inquiries and ministerial advisory groups. Its biennial Just Action conferences have become one of the major social-justice conferences in the country.

Not all aspects of the New Zealand SPPU's work are immediately transferable to other territories. It is possible, however, to draw some transferable lessons.

- The contribution The Salvation Army has to make in the formation of national social policy can be significant.

- The SPPU experience shows it is possible for The Salvation Army to be a provider of social services receiving government funding and still provide robust critique and criticism of government social policy. The exchange of views does often create tension. However, because there is sufficient reliable information, good relationships and a respect of differing positions, this tension allows for healthy debate and useful policy development.
- There is much to gain from non-fundraising relationships with private sector leaders.
- Community dialogue and changing the views of the general public using the Army's credibility can often be a vital step in the political process. The situations and views of the most vulnerable people can be given a new voice through The Salvation Army's work in a way that can lead government to change its social policy direction.

Responses to injustice are both situational and contextual. New Zealand is not Indonesia, Uganda, New Guinea or the United States. Still, the experiences of other territories provide promising practices that can spur initiatives which enhance the impact of ministry in our own countries.

~~~~

In my early days of ministry, I spent 18 years in some form of street ministry. I was in the trenches with others, listening to stories, working with service agencies, the church and government. The cry from much of society was to move the eyesores of social dysfunction from respectable locations to somewhere else that would be out of sight. The homeless were simply an embarrassment. The beggars were a nuisance. The alcoholics were bad for tourism. The prostitutes were deterrents to the best interests of local business enterprises.

On one occasion, two street-ministry workers from a team I directed were on a subway platform late at night in a major city. A mom and child got off the last train. They were 800 kilometres away from home, fleeing domestic violence. The mom saw the Salvation Army uniforms and started to walk towards them.

The six-year-old child held on to her mom's hand and listened as they talked. The story of domestic violence was at the centre of the crisis. A room for the night was the immediate concern. The Salvation Army was positioned to solve the immediate dilemma. Without fanfare or urgency, they moved toward emergency accommodation.

Along the way our Salvation Army staff engaged in conversation with the child and asked her name. She was not interested in the social niceties of the occasion. Her response had an edge: "I'm not homeless, I just don't have a place to put it!"

Those of us in The Salvation Army are often referred to as Good Samaritans. We are relentless in picking up victims in life on the roads of danger. But sometimes what we really need is to be stopped short on the Jericho Road and forced to ask whether our relief bandages are what is called for.

We don't know all that the six-year-old was trying to say in her statement. She could have had a long history of witnessing violence and running for cover. My point is this: in emergency situations, we hold social power. We are inclined to conclude that we know what is best. We are tempted to assume that here is another victim who will benefit from our diagnosis and prescription for therapy.—MCM

~~~~

Standing up and speaking out for justice for others means sticking your neck out far enough to risk calling attention to something beyond the immediate need. It can mean that offering an emergency night of safety is not enough. Rather than spending time writing a grant proposal for a contract extension, it means that we should be investing in research that leads to a policy change.

Sometimes we wear our Salvation Army uniforms as self-protective armour. Our ceaseless good deeds numb our sensitivities to the excruciating pain of systemic injustice. The protection and activism can keep us from being courageous enough to confront the economic and political decision makers who often appreciate us for the work we are doing. Knowing the afflictions of an unjust world needs to embolden us to stand up and speak out in the powerful places of our world. It is not enough for us to contain our compassion in our well-funded institutions of charity.

Our public branding means we have collateral to spend. Our international infrastructure positions us to be truly global. Our committed people are responsive to visionary leadership. Our bold conviction is ready to be expressed. Our readiness to seek God's direction will both protect us and inspire us. We have many opportunities. Where do we begin?

We value our public reputation, and we should. But in too many instances, have we surrendered our autonomy to what we want the media to project about us? Perhaps we have too readily agreed with them when they project the message: "The Salvation Army are the people who are ready to care for people who cannot care for themselves—the street people, the alcoholics, the prostitutes, the vagrants—the people that most people would like to ignore and don't care about. That is your defining place in the world. It's your special brand."

The issue is whether we can continue to be affirmed for our relentless compassion for the forgotten and the downtrodden while spending our collateral in more strategic ways for longer-term impact.

If we seek new opportunities and re-frame our mission, there are risks. Decidedly, we will need to exchange our fear of failure with a freedom to risk failing. We will dare to risk leaving the safety zones of our automatic renewal of government grants. We will grapple with the unknown. In new ways we will wrestle with what it means to live by faith.

Consequently, we will spend more time in the world. More of our personnel will develop skills to effectively engage government leaders and policy makers. We will be less insular and more involved with community leaders and other faith groups who share our concerns. We will stop being spectators on committees and token players at events. Praying invocations at public events will not be enough. Our drive will be to focus more outward and less inward.

Tragically, the poor too often learn to tolerate neglect and abuse because they think it's normal. They learn to keep a safe distance from the powerful instead of confronting them or collaborating with them for change. God has given The Salvation Army access to places and people who have social power. We have institutional collateral to invest in what is most important.

We can keep our Good Samaritan status and accept our awards for distinguished social service. And candidly, we should continue to do so. But the haunting question is—after close to 150 years of significant international history, is being a Good Samaritan really enough?

If justice is the measure of our ministry, the present scope of ministry and influence is not enough. If Isaiah's trumpet call is still a part of our fabric of faith, maintaining the status quo falls short.

The trumpet blast is not to wake up the unrighteous. It is directed at those of us who like to think of ourselves as God's preferred option. The prophet's chide is to get us out of the religious bunkers that isolate us from the battlefronts of despicable injustice.

No one who really understands us will ever criticize us for our lack of commitment. Our spiritual dedication is certain. We work hard. Our lives are marked with surrender to the Lord and The Salvation Army. But is that also part of our vulnerability? Instead of questioning, are we working at the right things, are we simply driven to work harder? Rather than stopping to reflect on our spiritual priorities, do we lapse into simply praying more and preaching louder?

Isaiah's trumpet call to "Shout out, do not hold back!" deserves our attention. Our historic commitment to address systemic causes of injustice invites us to assess our current ministry priorities. The prompting of the Holy Spirit that is mobilizing the broader church to pursue justice as an essential commitment of the gospel is evidence that our voice for justice has been too silent for too long.

CHAPTER 4

ADVOCATING FOR THE OPPRESSED

My brothers and sisters, do you with your acts of favouritism really believe in our glorious Lord Jesus Christ? For if a person with gold rings and in fine clothes comes into your assembly, and if a poor person in dirty clothes also comes in, and if you take notice of the one wearing the fine clothes and say, "Have a seat here, please," while to the one who is poor you say, "Stand there," or, "Sit at my feet," have you not made distinctions among yourselves, and become judges with evil thoughts? Listen, my beloved brothers and sisters. Has not God chosen the poor in the world to be rich in faith and to be heirs of the kingdom that he has promised to those who love him? But you have dishonoured the poor. Is it not the rich who oppress you? Is it not they who drag you into court? Is it not they who blaspheme the excellent name that was invoked over you?

You do well if you really fulfil the royal law according to the Scripture, "You shall love your neighbour as yourself." But if you show partiality, you commit sin (James 2: 1-9a).

Inconsistent behaviour in God's people tarnishes Christ's reputation. And by showing favouritism, particularly when we give preference to the rich at the expense of the poor, we damage Jesus' public image.

In Christ, there is equality of humanity. Whether we are high-school dropouts or PhD scholars, we all stand on level ground. Our worth is not calculated on the basis of having a bulging bank account or not having a mailing address to receive our welfare cheque.

The rich already have enough problems to deal with. Jesus said, it's spiritually dangerous to be rich. They can yield to the temptations of the abusive power of their money. It brings out the worst in them.

There is no merit in poverty, but the poor are more likely than the rich to see their need for God. Catering to the rich only makes them more vulnerable to their self-sufficiency.

Social discrimination is wrong. The poor are not to be shamed and the rich are not to be exalted. Love transcends favouritism.

God's royal law is what we should practise. When we love our neighbours as *neighbours*—even better, when we love our neighbours as brothers and sisters—be they poor or rich, we give evidence of our love for God.

The two most consequential factors in anyone's life are where you are born and who your family is. The profound influence of one's family and the inescapable impact of one's geography are enormous. Yet, no one has any control over either reality. Still, these two forces wield their power in determining people's economic status, social standing and spiritual destiny. If you are born into a Muslim or Christian family, in all probability you will embrace that Muslim or Christian religious identity. If you are born poor in a country that ranks on the bottom rungs of the human-development index, unless your family is economically privileged, your destiny sentences you to live in poverty.

This makes it sound as though people's lives are predetermined. Certainly, there are exceptions. Individuals can choose to reject their religious heritage or convert to another faith. Some who are born in poverty can advance their social standing. A few exceptions are able to transcend their beginnings and become the next generation of change-agent leaders. However, the majority of the world's seven billion people are bound by life's circumstances.

Why are people economically poor? Are they lazy? Intellectually inferior? Socially inept? Are the poor to be blamed for their plight or praised for their heroic efforts to survive? The response below is not complete but it is a beginning.

If you are born in Sierra Leone, Malawi, Burundi, Bangladesh, Haiti, Vietnam, Palestine or parts of Indonesia and India, your birthright most likely ensures that you are economically poor. Through no fault of your own, if you enter a caste-system culture without the privileges of being a member of a high caste, your lack of social standing will lead to deprivation and perpetual poverty. When people are forced to live without choices and resources, they suffer. Lack of access to education, health care, daily food and safe water hampers basic development and crushes the human spirit. Human potential is squandered and opportunities for meaningful employment are lost. Victims of abuse, corruption and violence also live in the grip of devastating poverty.

Turning a blind eye to the causal factors that victimize populations is not what is being proposed. Political corruption that channels wealth to abusive leaders must be stopped and penalized. Incompetent governance needs to be named and challenged. Repressive warlords must be restrained and removed from power. Leaders must be held responsible for the well-being of their people.

Still, overseas development funds need to be allocated to less-developed nations that can demonstrate quality program standards and accountability for performance. Regardless of the complexity, the prevailing global inequity between the more-developed and less-developed nations demands strategic and compassionate responses. Otherwise, we become indifferent to human-rights disgraces and content with systemic injustice.

Why are people spiritually poor? Are they inherently self-willed? Conditioned to be autonomous? Along the way, have they been damaged by their experiences with religion and religious people?

On the issue of spiritual poverty, we must be careful not to oversimplify what is profoundly complex. Still, there are primary and secondary causes. Many Christian theologians point back to the Garden of Eden and link spiritual poverty with an inherited human disposition for sin and disobedience. Who would deny that there is a human bias to be self-willed and autonomous?

In our search for the reasons of spiritual poverty, the questions of "Who is your family?" and "Where are you born?" are also predominant causal factors. The role of religion in every family is a strong indicator of how the next generation will respond to issues of faith. If parents are serious believers and live in ways that enrich the family's spiritual experience, the children will be influenced by their inheritance. The absence of family faith leaves children vulnerable and spiritually disadvantaged.

One's geographic and cultural inheritance is also a strong predictor for how people perceive the role of the spiritual in their lives. If you are born in an Islamic republic, in all likelihood you will be Muslim. Those born in the Philippines or South America will probably claim a Christian Catholic identity. In nations that have strong multi-faith populations or a predominance of Protestants and Catholics, the family background will play a strong role in how individuals establish and express their religious beliefs.

The absence of spiritual awareness can lead to lifelong journeys of spiritual poverty. Rejecting God's love, denying his truth and ignoring the consequences of sin are all detrimental to one's spiritual well-being.

The mission of Jesus is captured in a single vision with two dimensions. His hope for a restored humanity envisions well-being for people who are *spiritually poor* and people who are *socially poor*.

Advocating for the Poor

Jesus was an advocate for spiritual and social well-being. This was not an afterthought for Jesus, but rather the heart of his ministry. In his final days with his disciples, Jesus called himself an "advocate" and promised to send them another advocate, the Holy Spirit. The good news for all of us is that Jesus continues to advocate on our behalf:

"I am writing these things to you so that you may not sin. But if anyone does sin, we have an advocate with the Father, Jesus Christ the righteous" (1 John 2:1).

Encountering God in the Biblical Story

> *Resist the temptation to block out what may be different from your past understanding.*
> *Discern what is good and right so that your spiritual insight can guide your future aspirations.*

The following two passages contrast with each other. The first invites us to celebrate with the poor and the second obligates us to intentionally serve those who are hurting in various ways.

- If you are studying this book with a group, read the passage from Luke together out loud.
- Without commenting, take time to reflect privately on how you feel about the directive Jesus gave.
- Read the passage again silently. Write down your feelings and reactions.
- Without commenting, keep your notations to be shared after reading the second passage.
- Have someone read the passage from Matthew out loud.
- Read the passage a second time silently, especially noting the expression "Truly I tell you, just as you did it to one of the least of these who are members of my family, you did it to me."
- Write a paraphrase of what Jesus said that captures the meaning in your own words.

- Read your paraphrased statements to each other and discuss what you've learned.
- Return to your earlier comments on how you felt about being told to hold banquets for people who cannot return the favour. After engaging with the second passage, do you still feel the same way? Share your reflections with each other.

He said also to the one who had invited him, "When you give a luncheon or a dinner, do not invite your friends or your brothers or your relatives or rich neighbours, in case they may invite you in return, and you would be repaid. But when you give a banquet, invite the poor, the crippled, the lame, and the blind. And you will be blessed, because they cannot repay you, for you will be repaid at the resurrection of the righteous" (Luke 14:12-14).

When the Son of Man comes in his glory, and all the angels with him, then he will sit on the throne of his glory. All the nations will be gathered before him, and he will separate people one from another as a shepherd separates the sheep from the goats, and he will put the sheep at his right hand and the goats at the left. Then the king will say to those at his right hand, "Come, you that are blessed by my Father, inherit the kingdom prepared for you from the foundation of the world; for I was hungry and you gave me food, I was thirsty and you gave me something to drink, I was a stranger and you welcomed me, I was naked and you gave me clothing, I was sick and you took care of me, I was in prison and you visited me." Then the righteous will answer him, "Lord, when was it that we saw you hungry and gave you food, or thirsty and gave you something to drink? And when was it that we saw you a stranger and welcomed you, or naked and gave you clothing? And when was it that we saw you sick or in prison and visited you?" And the king will answer them, "Truly I tell you, just as you did it to one of the least of these who are members of my family, you did it to me." Then he will say to those at his left hand, "You that are accursed, depart from me into the eternal fire prepared for the devil and his angels; for I was hungry and you gave me no food, I was thirsty and you gave me nothing to drink, I was a stranger and you did not welcome me, naked and you did not give me clothing, sick and in prison and you did not visit me." Then they also will answer, "Lord, when was it that we saw you hungry or thirsty or a stranger or naked or sick or in prison, and did not take care of you?" Then he will answer them, "Truly I tell you, just as you did not do it to one of the least of these, you did not do it to me." And these will go away into eternal punishment, but the righteous into eternal life (Matthew 25:31-46).

The predicament of the poor was an ongoing concern in Jesus' life. Striking evidence of his bias for the poor was given during a visit to Simon the leper's home. A woman intruded on the conversation with a jar of expensive ointment in hand and began applying it to Jesus' head. Some of the guests suggested the money spent on the ointment should have been given to the poor instead. Jesus affirms the woman's good intentions and chides her critics: "For you always have the poor with you, and you can show kindness to them whenever you wish" (Mark 14:7). The incident highlights the difficult balance between spending money on celebrations and remembering the enduring needs of the poor.

Current Challenges

Both passages above underscore the mandate of Jesus to share resources with those who have less. But there is more to it than just being generous. Disregard for the needs of the poor is evidence of the absence of faith. A refusal to alleviate the pain of the poor in the here and now becomes the criterion for one's final judgment before God.

And that's not all. When followers of Jesus express their practical love, they also bring the touch of Christ into the lives of the poor. Christ is present when God's people are present and doing good is a practical expression of God's love.

The directive Jesus issued to express generosity to people who are not in a position to "pay you back" is a reminder to live beyond self-interest. Think about your community or city and some of your nearby neighbours whose needs exceed their limited resources. Is there a situation where you can offer to care for children so a single parent can have a night out? Can you tutor a struggling student, teach some vocational skills or influence your church to offer a compassionate service in your community?

On a global scale, the United Nations has proposed eight Millennium Development Goals (MDGs) as an overall strategy for addressing global poverty and social justice concerns.

1. Eradicate extreme poverty and hunger.
2. Achieve universal primary education.
3. Promote gender equality and empower women.
4. Reduce child mortality.
5. Improve maternal health.
6. Combat HIV-AIDS, malaria and other diseases.
7. Ensure environmental sustainability.
8. Develop a global partnership for development.[10]

Giving your attention to the less-developed world (sometimes referred to as the Third World), review the MDGs and identify what you consider to be the most critical issues of injustice that keep people from achieving their social and spiritual well-being.

Advocacy is a proven strategy for collectively addressing issues of poverty and injustice. The acrostic below captures components of effective advocacy. Review the framework.

ADVOCACY:
> **A**ddresses issues of injustice.
> **D**esigns strategies to alter systems.
> **V**alues vulnerable people as agents of change.
> **O**ffers expertise to implement objectives.
> **C**onvinces power structures to alter policies.
> **A**ccesses like-minded people to join the cause.
> **C**hanges policies, practices and perceptions.
> **Y**earns for justice that leads to sustainability.

Identify one of the advocacy components that captures your attention. Make an observation about your choice.

Let's be specific. Brainstorm how you and others might advocate to make a difference in response to the following issues:

Social Issue: Achieve universal primary education
One of the injustices in the less-developed world is access to "no-fee" primary education. Education is the best antidote to dead-end jobs,

perpetual dependence on welfare and living in poverty. What steps can be taken to close the education gap? Find out which relief and development organizations give priority to global education and choose one to support. Engage with government policy makers who are responsible for development assistance. Mobilize a local school to link with a school in the less-developed world and pursue what can be done together.

Spiritual issue: Freedom of religion

In the 1948 Universal Declaration of Human Rights, Article 18 affirmed: "Everyone has the right to freedom of thought, conscience and religion; this right includes freedom to change his/her religion or belief, and freedom, either alone or in community with others and in public or private, to manifest his/her religion or belief in teaching, practice, worship and observance."[11]

Get informed. Research and identify which countries have signed the Universal Declaration of Human Rights but do not practise the principles of religious freedom. Find out what organizations exist for the purpose of ensuring religious freedom. Align yourself with the efforts of an organization that inspires your confidence. Do something.

Prayers of Response

Close to home

Lord, we come to you again, thanking you for the modern prophets (musicians, politicians, religious leaders, benefactors) who have raised their voices on behalf of the poor. They are your advocates— your voices. In the midst of their appeals, we want to cry out that "charity" is not poor people's greatest need. The needs of the poor are the same as the needs of the privileged: good government, access to education, health care and social services, spiritual well-being, employment, a reliable judiciary, peace within their borders and choices that can lead to sustainability. God, equip us to engage in acts of compassion that result in sustainable justice. Amen.

Beyond our borders

Gracious God, in these times, may the world not grow tired of feeding the hungry, treating the sick and tutoring the illiterate. May those with resources design social programs that focus on cures instead of symptoms only. May those with political power implement strategic policies that alleviate the consequences of poverty while also eliminating its causes. The challenge is great. The progress is sporadic. The timelines are long. God help us. Amen.

Add your own specific prayers for those close to home and those beyond your borders.

Advocating for the Privileged

One might mistakenly assume that privileged people don't need advocates. After all, they have the resources and opportunities to make it on their own. Not so, in the mind of Jesus. For Jesus, the greatest spiritual vulnerability for all people— from all cultures and for all time—is self-sufficiency.

Self-sufficiency is enticing. Why be dependent when you can be independent? Why seek other people's counsel when you have all the answers yourself? Why wait in line when you can send a servant or employee to wait for you? Why worry about feeding your family when you can have a fridge full of food and choose whatever you want to eat? Why travel on a bus when you can fly first-class? Rather than worrying about the next loan payment, wouldn't you prefer to have investments and money in the bank? Who in their right mind would rather beg on the street than be ushered to a front-row seat to enjoy a concert?

Encountering God in the Biblical Story

There is a spiritual wind blowing in the following incidents.

The wind is gusty and storm-like with the rich ruler.

The breeze is gentle but troubling for Nicodemus.

Allow the breeze of the Spirit to catch your attention and keep you on course.

Be courageous enough to be truthful with yourself.

Desire the things of God and keep alert to the Spirit's whispers.

Read the rich ruler text silently on your own. Be patient; don't hurry.

- Read the story again on your own and identify one aspect in the scenario that especially catches your attention.
- Why did you focus on that particular aspect?
- If you are studying this book with a group, share your insight with the others.

A certain ruler asked him, "Good Teacher, what must I do to inherit eternal life?" Jesus said to him, "Why do you call me good? No one is good but God alone. You know the commandments: 'You shall not commit adultery; You shall not murder; You shall not steal; You shall not bear false witness; Honour your father and mother.'" He replied, "I have kept all these since my youth." When Jesus heard this, he said to him, "There is still one thing lacking. Sell all that you own and distribute the money to the poor, and you will have treasure in heaven; then come, follow me." But when he heard this, he became sad; for he was very rich. Jesus looked at him and said, "How hard it is for those who have wealth to enter the kingdom of God! Indeed, it is easier for a camel to go through the eye of a needle than for someone who is rich to enter the kingdom of God." Those who heard it said, "Then who can be saved?" He replied, "What is impossible for mortals is possible for God" (Luke 18:18-27).

- Read the Nicodemus text silently on your own. Take your time.
- Read the story again on your own and identify one aspect in the scenario that especially catches your attention.
- Why did you focus on that particular aspect?
- If you are studying this book with a group, share your insight with the others.

Now there was a Pharisee named Nicodemus, a leader of the Jews. He came to Jesus by night and said to him, "Rabbi, we know that you are a teacher who has come from God; for no one can do these signs that you do apart from the presence of God." Jesus answered him, "Very truly, I tell you, no one can see the kingdom of God without being born from above." Nicodemus said to him, "How can anyone be born after having grown old? Can one enter a second time into the mother's womb and be born?" Jesus answered, "Very truly, I tell you, no one can enter the kingdom of God without being born of water and Spirit. What is born of the flesh is flesh, and what is born of the Spirit is spirit. Do not be astonished that I said to you, 'You must be born from above.' The wind blows where it chooses, and you hear the sound of it, but you do not know where it comes from or where it goes. So it is with everyone who is born of the Spirit." Nicodemus said to him, "How can these things be?" Jesus answered him, "Are you a teacher of Israel, and yet you do not understand these things? Very truly, I tell you, we speak of what we know and testify to what we have seen; yet you do not receive our testimony. If I have told you about earthly things and you do not believe, how can you believe if I tell you about heavenly things? No one has ascended into heaven except the one who descended from heaven, the Son of Man. And just as Moses lifted up the serpent in the wilderness, so must the Son of Man be lifted up, that whoever believes in him may have eternal life. For God so loved the world that he gave his only Son, so that everyone who believes in him may not perish but may have eternal life" (John 3:1-16).

Money is always a big part of self-sufficiency. It is no wonder that Jesus was so direct on the issue: "Beware of the power of money!" was his warning. "No one can serve two masters; for a slave will either hate the one and love the other, or be devoted to the one and despise the other. You cannot serve God and wealth" (Matthew 6:24). Clearly, social hierarchy and economic disparity were also a part of life 2,000 years ago. Otherwise, there would have been no need for Jesus to include the above statement in the Sermon on the Mount.

The rich ruler was a self-sufficient member of society. He had wealth and was socially privileged. These benefits did not make him a bad person. There was a lot that was right about his intentions. His spiritual yearnings were admirable. His inner spirit desired to be right with God. Although he may have been self-centred, he followed the Old Testament commandments. When Jesus set the standard higher than the ruler was ready to accept, his response was sadness and remorse. Who could blame the man for wanting more? He already had as much of heaven on earth as anyone could have hoped for. Why didn't he add eternal life as the ultimate prize?

Nicodemus was also privileged—spiritually privileged. He was a Pharisee of high standing, a member of the Sanhedrin. Nicodemus was a scholar, a teacher of Israel with formal credentials. He was a man who was dedicated to God's law. Nicodemus provided answers to his people's religious questions. Still, he was like the rest of the

Israelites, who neither understood who Jesus was, nor accepted what Jesus asked them to believe.

Nicodemus had more outward credentials than Jesus, but his inner spirit was troubled. There was something about Jesus that was compelling to Nicodemus. He knew that Jesus was performing miracles and that his astonishing teachings were becoming controversial. Perhaps his discontent was linked with how he and his fellow Pharisees interpreted God's law. Whatever the motivation, in the quietness of the night, Nicodemus came to Jesus. They were two teachers in an intimate setting. But for Nicodemus, it was time to make himself vulnerable. It was time for him to be honest about his own spiritual questions.

Current Challenges

What you get ahold of gets ahold of you. What you embrace embraces you. In the rich ruler's case, he surrendered himself to the power of money and the privileges of wealth and social standing. Nicodemus sold his soul to the religious establishment. He embraced what he inherited. His ethnic culture and his religious rules and regulations propelled him into closed-system living. Both the rich ruler and Nicodemus were locked in the prisons of their privileges. Although they didn't see it at the time, Jesus was their advocate. Jesus was anxious to free them from the forces that oppressed them.

In the case of the rich ruler, money and social prominence fuelled his sense of self-sufficiency. When we perceive ourselves to be self-sufficient, we become our own authorities. We self-construct our values, morals and beliefs. We set our own priorities, let personal prerogative drive our decision making, and have the final word on what is right and wrong. We think we know what is best. But our presumed strength blinds us to our need for God. In the rich ruler's case, he exchanged the God of creation for the god of money.

- Identify the influences in your life that nurture your self-sufficiency and autonomy. Think about Jesus' intentions with the rich ruler. If you are studying this book with a group, discuss with the others.

• What do you think Jesus was trying to achieve? What do you understand about God's intentions for you and others?

For whatever reasons, Nicodemus' religious system was disrupted. He was no longer an answering machine. In fact, his answers turned into questions that troubled him. The response Jesus gave to Nicodemus was that his present spiritual assumptions were inadequate and incomplete. There was more for him to discover and experience. "Nicodemus, no one can see the kingdom of God without being born from above ... you must be born again."

Nicodemus had difficulty understanding what Jesus meant. How do you understand the meaning of "being born from above" or "being born again"? Without using those particular expressions, write a personal paraphrase that expresses what they mean to you. If you are studying this book with a group, discuss your statements.

Evangelism and Christian witness at their best are expressions of spiritual advocacy. Jesus helped us understand the role of the Holy Spirit when he told Nicodemus, "The wind blows where it chooses, and you hear the sound of it, but you do not know where it comes from or where it goes. So it is with everyone who is born of the Spirit." What can we learn from this teaching about how people come to Christ and experience salvation?

There are two subsequent references to Nicodemus and his response to Jesus. In John 7:45-52, Nicodemus becomes an advocate for Jesus with his Pharisee colleagues. Following the Crucifixion, Nicodemus brought a hundred pounds of myrrh and aloes to care for Jesus' body (see John 19:38-42). It seems fair to conclude that Nicodemus became a believer and a follower.

Prayers of Response

Close to home
Our God, we are inclined to equate our material riches and preferred social standing as evidence of your blessing. Nicodemus and the rich ruler remind us that we should fear neglecting our spiritual poverty. Lord, we wonder why we are so enamoured with our pursuit of self-sufficiency. We know we are weak but we insist on pretending we are

strong. Why are we so ambivalent—so pulled by self-interest and still ready to let you rein us in? We have not forgotten that you created us but that you do not coerce us. Please God, do not let us stray too far. Keep us close enough to your presence so that our self-interest will be more and more fused with your interests. Amen.

Beyond our borders

Our God, gather together people of conscience and conviction to respond to both the spiritual and social needs of people everywhere. Give them a passion for the possible. Instil visions in them to make inhumane places more humane. Inspire in them the ways and means that create opportunities for people to sustain their lives with dignity. Wherever these principled people live and whatever they believe, give them a sense that they are a part of your vision to pursue justice, love mercy and walk humbly with the God who created them. Amen.

Add your own specific prayers for those close to home and those beyond your borders.

Releasing the Oppressed

Many people are uncomfortable at the mere mention of demons. These same people may acknowledge a spiritual world of some kind, but they doubt the existence of demons. Ironically, these people subscribe to horoscopes, the occult and psychics but have no place for the powers and principalities of the devil. Angels maybe, but demons never.

Many of God's people are comfortable assuming that we live in a spirit world where forces of good and evil co-mingle and wrestle with each other. In their world view, Satan is the evil one, the prince of demons. Principalities and powers do create darkness in the core of the human soul, and those who are empowered by God to exorcise and cast demons out in the name of Jesus are applauded.

Encountering God in the Biblical Story

Accept God's gift of spiritual nourishment.

Pray for enough energy to live faithfully through another hour, another day, another week.

Strive to live fully through another disagreement, another disappointment, another surprise.

There are two sections in the passage from the first chapter of Mark cited here. The first takes place in public, in the synagogue. The second begins in a private home with four of the disciples. In both situations, miraculous healings are the outcome.

- If you are studying this book as a group, listen carefully as both sections are read aloud.
- Allowing your attention to focus on a particular aspect of the story, read the passage silently.
- Take time to reflect on what has grasped your attention.
- Interact with each other and share what you are hearing and thinking.

They were astounded at his teaching, for he taught them as one having authority, and not as the scribes. Just then there was in their synagogue a man with an unclean spirit, and he cried out, "What have you to do with us, Jesus of Nazareth? Have you come to destroy us? I know who you are, the Holy One of God." But Jesus rebuked him, saying, "Be silent, and come out of him!" And the unclean spirit, convulsing him and crying with a loud voice, came out of him. They were all amazed, and they kept on asking one another, "What is this? A new teaching— with authority! He commands even the unclean spirits, and they obey him." At once his fame began to spread throughout the surrounding region of Galilee. As soon as they left the synagogue, they entered the house of Simon and Andrew, with James and John. Now Simon's mother-in-law was in bed with a fever, and they told him about her at once. He came and took her by the hand and lifted her up. Then the fever left her, and she began to serve them. That evening, at sundown, they brought to him all who were sick or possessed with demons. And the whole city was gathered around the door. And he cured many who were sick with various diseases, and cast out many demons; and he would not permit the demons to speak, because they knew him (Mark 1:22-34).

In the Luke 4 passage that follows, we have returned to where we started in the introduction to this series. It is early in Jesus' public ministry. He is back home speaking at the synagogue where he learned and worshipped as a child. And it is here that he explains his mission on earth in what we have called his "inaugural address." In the Mark passage above, people have been miraculously freed from evil spirits and the oppression of physical sickness. In the Luke 4 passage, Jesus sets his sights on other forms of oppression. He has good news for those who are blind to their predicaments and captive to the "anti-God forces" in their lives.

- If you are studying this book as a group, read the Luke 4 passage out loud together.
- Read the passage silently on your own.
- Scan the passage again and identify a central thought.
- Write down your observations.
- Share your perceptions with members of your group and connect what God is saying to them with your own impressions.

When he came to Nazareth, where he had been brought up, he went to the synagogue on the sabbath day, as was his custom. He stood up to read, and the scroll of the prophet Isaiah was given to him. He unrolled the scroll and found the place where it was written: "The Spirit of the Lord is upon me, because he has anointed me to bring good news to the poor. He has sent me to proclaim release to the captives and recovery of sight to the blind, to let the oppressed go free, to proclaim the year of the Lord's favour." And he rolled up the scroll, gave it back to the attendant, and sat down. The eyes of all in the synagogue were fixed on him. Then he began to say to them, "Today this scripture has been fulfilled in your hearing" (Luke 4:16-21).

The Bible refers to demons 70 different times. Only two of these references occur in the Old Testament. Jesus repeatedly freed people from the presence and power of their inner demons. Images of light and darkness and struggles between good and evil frequently dramatize the pages of Scripture.

The two biblical passages above reveal that demons' many manifestations can create common consequences. Demons are oppressive. They invade the human spirit. They are seductive and haunting. They are deceptive, coercive and controlling. They are spiritually destructive. Best understood, "demons of the soul" are the anti-God forces in our lives.

Current Challenges

Belief in demons and their devastating power is more prevalent in some church denominations and in particular regions of the world. Consequently, when charismatic churches preach a "powers and principalities" understanding of the gospel, high-voltage worship is celebrated. In some of the less-developed countries in the world, the poor are often rich in faith. Where access to medical care is limited, a more profound dependence on God seems to be evident. Prayer is powerful and there are expectations that miracles of healing will win the day.

Assess how your church community deals with "demons" and the need for miracles to counter and conquer these "powers and principalities." What is your personal perspective?

For centuries, Christians have identified a list of seven "deadly sins" that, for our purposes, can be understood as "demons of the soul" or "anti-God forces" in our lives. The historical list includes lust, gluttony, greed, sloth, wrath, envy and pride. Think about your society, your country, your community.

From the "deadly sins" list, identify two that you think have the most devastating effect on life around you. How would life be different if they no longer existed?

Consider the consequences of another demon on the soul, the anti-God force of refusing to forgive. Refusal to forgive is like a death sentence. It's a self-imposed state of oppression. In contrast, forgiveness releases people to deal with the past and find a pathway into the future.

Imagine a world without forgiveness. Discuss the consequences. Now imagine a world where forgiveness could be spread in war zones, gifted to fractured families, injected into dysfunctional workplaces, infused into individuals who are locked in past memories and unable to begin again.

Give your attention to one other devastating demon of the soul: the anti-God force of selfishness. If God is love and God's great command is to love, then selfishness is the greatest life-denying, oppression-inflicting, injustice-creating force in our world. Selfishness is catastrophic.

Selfishness restricts life to the boundary of self-interest and imprisons people within their own little worlds. Selfishness damages people in the swath of its desires, denies justice and the rights of others, and ignores those victimized by poverty. Selfishness excludes the marginalized.

Tragically, selfishness blinds its victims to a life worth living.

Love, on the other hand, is life-giving. To live is to love and to love is to live. It is God's love and God's love in us that advocates boldly for the vulnerable and the unlovable.

The ethic of love refuses to muzzle the truth. The principle of love includes the excluded. The emotion of love inspires creativity, generosity and risk. The morality of love seeks justice for all. The boundaries of love are set far beyond self-interest.

Fortunately, there is more love in God than there is selfishness in us.

Prayers of Response

Close to home

Our God, forgive me for the many times that selfishness has crowded out my awareness of others. I confess that I have been so occupied with me that I have been blind to their predicaments. Help me to see more clearly. Enable me to resist the demons in my soul that deny you access to my brokenness. Lord, free all of us from those enemies of our souls that oppress us, those addictions, those light and darkness struggles that cripple us. Free us from all those anti-God forces that divert your life-giving energy from our hungry spirits. Amen.

Beyond our borders

Our God, the world you have created exceeds the reach of our comprehension. There is more diversity that we can embrace, more beauty than we can imagine and more darkness than the sun can chase away. As the sun rises in your worldwide creation today, we pray that light will be more evident than darkness, demons of the soul will lose their power and injustice will be stifled. We pray that the spirit of the Lord will reign, oppression will limp into the sunset and justice will prevail. Amen.

Add your own specific prayers for those close to home and those beyond your borders.

The Salvation Army Story: Favouring the Unfavoured

Social discrimination is wrong. The poor are not to be shamed and the rich are not to be exalted. Love transcends favouritism.

God's royal law is what we should practise. When we love our neighbours as ourselves—even better, when we love our neighbours as "brothers and sisters"—be they poor or rich, we give evidence of our love for God (James 2:7-9, paraphrase).

In this world, there are the favoured and the unfavoured, the privileged and the impoverished.

Where and when a person is born, who their parents are and what talents mark their human capacity have inescapable consequences. It's like a "natural lottery." Life begins without choices. There are givens. The enduring question is what do we do with our human inheritance? What do I do with my givens? The question applies to both individuals and society. "How should society's decision makers steward our shared givens?"

If we enter life among the favoured, will we use that fact to cozy up to the even more favoured? Or will we turn to help the less favoured? And if we turn towards them, with what attitude will we express our intentions? If, on the other hand, we begin life as one of the unfavoured, will we be content to find just our individual success? How will we define the "success" we seek?

James, the brother of Jesus, wrote to a church that struggled with being socially just. It wanted status and gave preference to the wealthy. It made room for the poor, but only grudgingly. What was James to say? What would you say?

~~~~

When I was a child, one of my toys was an inflatable globe. My father would blow up the globe and take me on adventures. Sometimes we would go to the beach or visit a friend. He always expanded my world. The inflated globe took me to continents and their countries. I learned about customs and languages and had dreams of places to visit in the future.

The world that unfolded in my emerging childhood was the shape of things to come. In 2007, while I was the leader of The Salvation Army in my home territory of Canada and Bermuda, I received a call from General Shaw Clifton, then the Army's international leader. He outlined his dream for a Salvation Army that would consider social justice as an entry point for our transformational mission. The International Social Justice Commission (or "ISJC" as we affectionately call it) would be the prime vehicle. "I would not wish anyone to think that the Army has been uninvolved hitherto in matters of social justice or social action," he said at the public dedication of the ISJC. "Far from it—but the creation of the Commission gives a renewed, modern focus to it all and provides a previously missing element of intentional co-ordination across the lands in which currently we work." Partnering with United Nations-related agencies was part of my mandate as the Commission's head. "It is expected that the International Social Justice Commission will expand and develop the Army's role and influence with the United Nations."[12]

The Salvation Army has had a civil-society presence in some form or other at the United Nations since its founding in 1948. In fact, in some ways The Salvation Army was already eagerly awaiting the UN's arrival. In the 1933 Salvation Army Year Book, Commissioner Carvosso Gauntlett wrote, "Salvationists are among the most ardent supporters of the League of Nations, and sincerely hope that it may achieve much and lasting good…. Salvationists, whatever their social or educational standing, almost inevitably think internationally."[13]

Since 2007, the ISJC staff has spent many days at the United Nations. Challenged to walk the maze of its organizational structure, we have attuned our ears to hear the talking points that incite indignation and joined hands with those willing to confront inequity. —MCM

~~~

The United Nations is imperfect and easy to criticize. Still, one of its strengths is to be a global stage for interaction between the favoured and the unfavoured. In 2000, 189 member states of the UN asked the question, "What can be done to eradicate poverty?" They settled on eight measurable Millennium Development Goals that would tackle the edge-of-death existence facing the world's "bottom billion." The year 2015 was targeted as the date to reach significant achievements. Although the MDGs were cited earlier in this section of the book, they merit being re-stated.

1. Eradicate extreme poverty and hunger.
2. Achieve universal primary education.
3. Achieve gender equality and empower women.
4. Reduce child mortality.
5. Improve maternal health.
6. Combat HIV-AIDS, malaria and other diseases.
7. Ensure environmental sustainability.
8. Develop a global partnership for development.

The Salvation Army has an array of program initiatives that are addressing the stated MDGs to eradicate extreme poverty and hunger. One example is the WORTH-saving programs. In Kenya, Tanzania and Uganda, women are taking the lead by acquiring skills to read and write, generating personal and group savings, creating successful small businesses and becoming bankers in their own right.

Micro-credit programs are making a difference in India, China, Zambia, Indonesia and Sri Lanka. Food programs are impacting Malawi, Uganda and India.

Achieving universal primary education is being addressed through schools and literacy programs in India, Uganda, Tanzania, Zimbabwe, Bolivia, Ecuador, Peru, Chile, Indonesia, Korea, China, Malaysia and Singapore.

Home leagues in every less-developed country and anti-sexual trafficking programs in China, Sri Lanka, Ecuador and Eastern Europe promote gender equality and empower women.

Community health programs in South Africa, Zambia, Zimbabwe, Democratic Republic of Congo, Republic of Congo,

Ghana, Bolivia, Ecuador, India, Indonesia and Bangladesh work both to reduce child mortality and improve maternal health.

A variety of programs in every territory in Africa, India, Indonesia, Bangladesh, Sri Lanka, China, South Korea and Eastern Europe combat AIDS, malaria and other diseases. Awareness and training programs are being set up to help establish a global partnership for development.

Measurable progress is being achieved. It might not be complete justice for the poor, but some justice is better than no justice. "Proximate justice" is to be celebrated and the quest for more is being sustained.

~~~~

When William Booth wrote *In Darkest England and the Way Out*, the urban poor of London, England, lived inhumanly. "Every cab horse in London has three things: a shelter for the night, food for its stomach, and work allotted to it by which it can earn its corn. These are the two points of the Cab Horse's Charter. When he is down he is helped up, and while he lives he has food, shelter and work. That, although a humble standard, is at present absolutely unattainable by millions of our fellow men and women in this country." [14]

Horses in William Booth's day were given more respect than human beings. It wasn't right. It wasn't fair. It was outrageous! As Booth and others proved, however, it also wasn't a necessary fate. The givens into which people were born could be altered, and they were. England still has too many people who struggle with poverty, but there are social protections now where none existed a century ago.

~~~~

A similar social justice story involves the Lamprell Street match factory. In 19th-century England, fires had to be lit for the basics of daily living. Electric lights, stoves and furnaces were yet to be invented, so matches were a necessary commodity. The most common matches were made using yellow phosphorus. Tragically, the phosphorus poisoned numbers of workers in the match-making industry. The chemical would get on their hands and if they ate without first washing their hands, the result was "phossy jaw." Often the necrosis of the tissues resulted in loss of teeth and disfigurement of the jaw. Sometimes, even death was the consequence. For their efforts, the workers were paid a pittance. Having little education, few employment skills and no legal protection by way of workplace health and safety regulations, they couldn't do much about their situation on their own.

William Booth took action. A factory building on Lamprell Street in East London was purchased and renovated. In May 1891, The Salvation Army opened a "state of the art" match factory. The manufacturing process was totally free of the toxic phosphorus and the employees were paid up to 60 percent more than the prevailing industry standard.

"Darkest England matches," as they were known, came to the attention of prominent Britons. Canon Wilberforce recommended them to his congregation in a sermon he preached in Westminster Abbey. Even the prime minister of the day, W.E. Gladstone, became a customer.

In 1901, the factory was taken over by the British Match Company.[15] The intent never had been for The Salvation Army to stay in the business of making and marketing matches. It took 10 years to create a new industry standard and then the Army got out, but in those 10 years, it showed there was a better and more just way.

"Phossy jaw" may be a thing of the past, but the exploitation of workers continues. One might ask, "Where are the advocates now?"

~~~~

Part of the problem with successful justice ventures is that they become ends in themselves. The injustice of one day is faced head on. Egregious wrongs are righted. "Temporal salvation," as Booth called it, comes to one group of oppressed people, and all of this gives us cause for great celebration. But then what? Do those who are served take up the cause for others still less favoured?

Our Salvation Army corps work faces some similar challenges. A church of the poor is transformed in a process that has been popularized as "redemption and lift." Founding members of the corps, who were poor and uneducated and perhaps saddled with self-destructive addictions, get saved and their lives are thoroughly changed spiritually and temporally. They pass on their transformation to their children and grandchildren. The children meet the same Saviour their parents met, and they also have better education, better jobs and better social standing. Then the grandchildren, building on what previous generations have gifted them, feel out of place in the poorer part of town and decide the corps should move to the suburbs where they all now live.

No one would want it otherwise for parents, children and grandchildren. Justice improves the conditions of life. Who wouldn't want to thrive? The question is whether justice for some can become justice for more. Once yesterday's oppression has been advocated for, and the less favoured have become the more favoured, the "pursue more justice" cycle often stops.

We are left needing new advocates.

~~~

Vânia Batista, the daughter of Salvation Army officers, lives in Niterói, Brazil, on the edge of Rio de Janiero. She completed social work studies at university in 2000 and married Leonardo Quintão, a lawyer and soldier at the corps. Young professionals with lots going for them, they have been involved in the corps' activity ever since.

Between 2003 and 2006, Vânia started to feel uncomfortable with religious activities practised only within the corps' four walls. In 2006, she was invited by The Salvation Army to participate in a youth camp in Córdoba, Argentina, focused on training young people in integrated mission principles. The occasion gave Vânia the opportunity to think about her own reality in Niterói. She set up an action plan for when she returned home.

The focus of her concern related to the female, male and transgendered commercial sex workers active in the area of the corps' hall. There were numerous churches in the area surrounding where the prostitutes worked but the congregations seemed to be indifferent to what was happening. Vânia was troubled. In her heart, she saw no Christian values and practices that had been taught during the integrated mission camp. She felt that her own corps was out of step with The Salvation Army's calling.

The challenges began as soon as she returned to her community and corps. She found that there was no interest on the part of corps leaders to be involved. At the time, Vânia and her husband, Leonardo, were leaders of the youth group. Using their access and influence, they began sharing their passion for community-based advocacy. As a group the youth began to analyze the reality around them with the intention of expressing their call to mission within their community.

The benign neglect from others in the corps became vocal opposition. The youth group began to suffer from the negative response to their "new ideas." Sensitive to the situation, Vânia told the young people not to do anything their leaders would not approve of. Accordingly, they scaled back their initiative and decided they would simply go and walk the streets at night to observe and pray. Would the full dream ever be born?

At the end of 2007, a new couple were appointed as the corps officers in Niterói. In God's providence they were already sympathetic to integrated mission principles. With their blessing, in July 2008, a seminar on integrated mission was held. A teacher who specializes in the subject came from the Presbyterian university and the whole corps was encouraged to attend. The sessions included a nurse talking about sexually transmitted diseases, a lawyer speaking about human rights and justice, and Vânia speaking about working with the community. Eighteen people came to listen and 13 got involved. The resulting "Open Doors" project allows people to safely walk the streets of Niterói's town centre and relate to those involved in commercial sex.

Vânia and the project team members took a number of steps. They began by emphasizing the idea that The Salvation Army has been there in the community many years. Still, they did not know the resident population and needed to do so. They took initiative and the commercial sex workers agreed to be surveyed to allow the Salvationists to get to know their main concerns. Relationships were deepened along the way. The offer of free jeans, T-shirts and a basket full of chocolates caught the sex workers' attention. Some were surprised, but the gesture of friendship was a signal of a desire to build a relationship.

The situation continues to develop. Members of Open Doors have visited homes and participated in people's lives. Mutual understanding is building bridges of trust. Empathy is extended in response to the dangers and the humiliation that people face on the streets. The story is unfinished but small victories bring the promise of more to come.

There are still soldiers in the corps who say that if the prostitutes come into the hall they will leave! We are reminded that repositioning for social justice will not be easy work. But the alternative is not to walk away from the justice mission.

~~~

We will make progress when we build solidarity among those who have a vision to be advocates. Let's learn from and teach others. Let's pass along the wisdom of our experiences. We know there is no recipe. But we also know that time-tested frameworks can help frame thinking and guide strategy.

Recall the ADVOCACY acrostic, developed by the ISJC, that was introduced a few pages ago. Ponder its application.

ADVOCACY
Addresses issues of injustice.
Designs strategies to alter systems.
Values vulnerable people as agents of change.
Offers expertise to implement objectives.
Convinces power structures to alter policies.
Accesses like-minded people to join the cause.
Changes policies, practices and perceptions.
Yearns for justice that leads to sustainability.

In the context of communities in the less-developed world where needs exceed resources, the advocacy process usually happens in stages. The progress from dependency to independence and sustainability normally takes many initiatives over a number of years. Typically, the following stages are marks of progress:

1. Advocate FOR others—outside voices addressing issues of injustice.
2. Advocate WITH others—valuing inside voices as agents of change.
3. Advocate FOR YOURSELVES—local justice initiatives that lead to sustainability.

~~~~

Major events in the General Assembly of the United Nations in New York are always impressive. While the ambassadors and dignitaries sit at desks bearing their nations' names, representatives from the ISJC often get invited to observe from the balcony. On this occasion, the MDGs were the topic. In walked the secretary general and the president of the United Nations. The president brought the assembly to order by hitting the gavel on the wide marble top of the lectern. Then he asked an unusual question: "May a child speak in the assembly this morning?" Nods of assent went around the auspicious body and a boy of 11 was asked to come to the podium.

He was unseen as the lectern blocked his tiny body from view, so a box was secured. Now properly "elevated," our speaker was ready to address the assembly. For 20 minutes this child spoke as an advocate for hunger relief.

The one difference in the great assembly hall that day was that the advocate did not read from books, papers on research or cite the latest statistics. He was the subject himself—he told his story of hunger pangs and fear that his life would end before he had a chance to really live. When he was finished, the assembly erupted, stood to their feet with cheers, tears and extended applause.

On that day, an 11-year-old was an advocate for the cause of food security. He spoke for himself and others who shared his plight, and he challenged world leaders to work together to create a more just world.
—MCM

~~~~

Undoing oppression can be such strenuous work that the importance of sustainability gets lost. The Old Testament story of the Hebrew people illustrates the point. The Hebrew slaves rejoiced when Moses led them away from Pharaoh and landed them on the safe side of the Red Sea. But it took a generation before the freed slaves became free citizens. Freedom from slavery needed to become freedom for self-rule. The journey was long.

"Full salvation"—a Salvation Army phrase that has regrettably gone out of fashion—is freedom from the demons of both spiritual and worldly oppression. It refuses to polarize "temporal salvation" with its strain of daily struggle against the hope of the richness of life with God forever. It strains for fullness of life forever, beginning now.

Like the Hebrews of old, we live in an imperfect here-and-now world. But we do so longing for freedom from injustice for those who live with deep human need. Life is meant to be more than simply surviving. The cries of our heads and hearts are that people would be able to live justly. Rather than eking out life in order to live another day, our vision is that people will flourish—that their environments would contribute to their God-given potential.

Seeking to contribute to a more just world, The Salvation Army ISJC has set itself five strategic goals:

1. Raise strategic voices to advocate with the world's poor and oppressed.
2. Be a recognized centre of research and critical thinking on issues of global social justice.
3. Collaborate with like-minded organizations to advance the global cause of social justice.
4. Exercise leadership in determining social justice policies and practices of The Salvation Army.
5. Live the principles of justice and compassion and inspire others to do likewise.

When we tell social justice stories from the past and present, we are amplifying strategic voices as advocates for a world that can be more fair. We are also demonstrating that social change most often happens as a result of collaboration between the favoured and the unfavoured. Vulnerable people have the capacity to be agents of change but progress is more likely when the voices of the vulnerable are also championed by people with organizational and social power.

The two roles are meant to complement each other. Individual involvement reminds us that every social issue has a human face. No one knows more about their situation than the person living in the predicament. When our awareness is person specific, individuals do not get lost in the pursuit of the cause, and neither do they face the risk of being tokenized or patronized.

Mission-driven organizations can bring social leverage to the table. They can more readily access policy makers and influence their decisions for the collective good. They can also make a place at the table for the voices of the marginalized. However, being favoured in this world also has its vulnerabilities. It is tempting for those with position and power to control the agenda—to determine the terms on which others sit with them and set the conditions on which they may speak. Parameters need to be set that protect the recipients of their good work from being marketed as trophies.

~~~

Arriving by air in Mizoram, a state in the northeast of India, I was met by my Salvation Army hosts. They were gracious but also apologetic. The journey from the airport was to have taken 45 minutes but the bridge had collapsed that week and the main highway was blocked. My driver was struggling to escape the airport on the secondary road. "Do you get car sick?" he asked, and I realized the secondary road was going to be an adventure.

Sure enough the hairpin turns and mountain-edge views required a strong constitution. The scenery was spectacular until we began to enter the villages of roughly constructed houses on stilts poised precariously over the mountain's edge. Then I saw the impoverished villagers. They were carrying firewood and attempting to sell precious food items along the side of the road. In my mind I knew they were parents with hopes that their children would have opportunities for more.

I asked the local leader of The Salvation Army about what I was seeing. I was informed that many of the residents were refugees from neighbouring Myanmar. In their stark reality, they were trying to make a living by any means.

In one of the surrounding villages, The Salvation Army had begun holding worship services that attracted many from the community. They heard the gospel and responded positively to accept Jesus as their Saviour and friend. However, their newfound faith created a problem. They were people who made their livelihood by brewing and selling bootleg alcohol. Now that they were Christians, they became convicted that they needed to change their ways. The change was costly. Their conscience told them that their practices were harmful to others and dangerous to themselves. However, a second problem emerged: alternative work was not forthcoming and their poverty was deepening.

As I boarded my plane to leave Mizoram, my spirit was troubled. I thought about my years working with alcoholics and the isolation of sobriety that haunted those brave people who said "no" to their addiction. I wondered how the new Mizo converts would cope. I struggled with a theory of Christian faith that was throwing families with children into the tumult of unemployment and empty kitchens.

In that moment, if justice is the measure of our ministry, I knew we had to do more. In order for the unfavoured to become more favoured, the present status quo is inadequate. We need to stop taking away life that was feasible without offering alternatives to live respectfully. We need to do more with micro-enterprise ventures. We need to do more about lobbying governments and proposing policy innovations that benefit the unfavoured. We need to empower the disadvantaged to speak with confidence about their predicaments. As the international Salvation Army, we need to be more global. Our more-developed territories need to share more of their resources with our less-developed territories. We need to pursue a sustainable justice that brings more of heaven to earth. I became convinced that we cannot continue to pray, "Your kingdom come, your will be done on earth as it is in heaven," without doing more—a lot more!—MCM

CHAPTER 5

I HEAR A CALL IN THE NIGHT:
A Personal Reflection From
M. Christine MacMillan

*A*s a young Salvation Army captain just having been moved to *London, England, from Canada, M. Christine MacMillan dared to request a short-term appointment prior to taking up the territorial headquarters assignment that had been the Army's primary reason for the move. Her request was to live and work in the women's hostel called Hopetown. Her intent was to have some grassroots experience in the east end of London where The Salvation Army had its beginnings.*

Living in the hostel, I found myself walking the neighbourhood of early-day Salvationists who preached in tents, dance halls and on street corners.

On one of my rambles I came across a statue. The figure, located in the neighbourhood of the poorest postal code in London, turned out to be William Booth. The monument had known more perfect days. Booth's broken fingers served as hooks for people in the community to hang beer bottles and "take out boxes" from the local fast food eatery.

Their creativity caused me to smile.

Viewing the statue also saddened my spirit. The cold hardness of the statue lacked the warmth of Booth's compassion. The broken hands reminded me that as impressive as his impact had been, the conditions in the neighbourhood were still a nightmare for so many. I wondered if some of Booth's original vision had gone silent—like trying to get blood out of a stone.

When I was appointed as the first director of The Salvation Army's International Social Justice Commission, I felt both a reluctance and a longing for new adventures. Prior to departing for New York City to take up my new role, I was to speak in Vancouver.

There was a twist to the request. I was heading to a new global appointment but ironically, I was going back to Vancouver, where I had started my Salvation Army mission. The congregation's request was that I speak about my future ministry.

The task felt overwhelming. I wanted to communicate some passion for what was at the time only a job description on paper. With a pen in hand I went back and forth attempting to carve a talk and it was almost midnight when I determined that my Saturday night required sleep before a busy Sunday. But my mind would not go to sleep. Tossing in the night, I turned on the radio to a late-night talk show. Drifting off, I awoke a few hours later to what for me was an unusual atmosphere. There was a presence of angelic voices singing a song that sounded familiar. Rousing myself out of my sleep, I realized the talk show was off the air and music was emanating from the speaker. I was not in heaven, but the lyrics of the song sat me up in bed with a startled recognition of my future:

> Here am I, Lord,
> It is I, Lord,
> I can hear you calling in the night.

That's when I said, "My future ministry is confirmed. The NIGHT CALL IS MY CALL." I turned on the light and rewrote my talk. I was like Jacob who struggled and wrestled through the night while asleep on a stone pillow. Little did I know that "stone pillows" would be part of my night's work.

Night calls are often God's way of waking us up. Recall young Samuel asleep in the temple and called no less than three times. What he thought was Eli's priestly seasoned voice was actually another's. Yet, Samuel received sound counsel from his fatherly mentor, Eli: "If the voice comes again, Samuel, here's your answer: 'Yes, Lord, your servant is listening.'" Listening to God's message was one thing and delivering it was another. Messages which eventually went from Samuel as prophet to his Israelite community were going to create their own demands.

For the last number of years, God has been speaking to me about the darkness in our world that is breaking his heart. Having lived and visited London on multiple occasions, it is not unusual for me to find myself entering churches of historic renown. Inscriptions over doorways and other places often capture my attention. When visiting Exeter Cathedral, I read a statement that is as challenging now as the day I first read it.

"Justice can only be effective if those who are not affected
feel as much indignation as those who are."
Solon of Athens 638-559 BC

Solon of Athens tells us that grappling with justice coincides with both our historical and present tense existence. His prescription for effectiveness resides in our inner spirits—in how we view the state of the well-being of others. He asserts that emotional indignation is the informed human response to injustice. Accordingly, if my faith journey does not feel disturbed by the state of today's world, then I have been victimized by spiritual indifference. I have become numb to the pain of others and shut down my capacity to sense indignation.

Feeling indignation is heightened when education and research enable us to explore the depths of injustice at its root. When I walk into a speaking engagement equipped with information about an issue of injustice, my knowledge base does not necessarily win the day. Participants in the audience are forming judgments as to the whys and wherefores on the nature and causes of injustice. I have learned to keep my opinions to myself early in the debate. Exploring the principles of our biblical justice material has not always won the day. Some people choose to hold on to views that keep captives enslaved and blamed. My own indignation rises when the church writes off justice as some secular poisoning of church doctrine. I have been left wondering: Why is it so difficult for some people to embrace a God who loves justice and sense his heart breaking in the very places that cry out for him?

The Salvation Army is known in many countries as the biggest charity next to the government. We are trusted to carry out charitable acts of kindness when others invest with sizable and consistent donations. The track record of the Army is supernatural.

Compassion moves us to punch well above our weight. Millions of individuals every year have been touched by The Salvation Army, and in most cases look at us with respect and gratitude. What would be the impact if we heightened the importance of seeking justice into our actions and reputations?

Our heritage in The Salvation Army is predicated on our desire to serve God with clean hands and pure hearts. We call this holiness. A tidy righteousness is tempting these days in the complexities of injustice. But as a friend of mine has reminded me: life is messy; graveyards are tidy.

The fourth doctrine of The Salvation Army states Jesus is "truly and properly God and truly and properly man." The studies that have woven their way through this book portray Jesus as an advocate for justice. What is certain is that Jesus' example of seeking justice coincides with The Salvation Army's historic and continuing commitment to justice. Living as a marginal member of his society, Jesus was a justice activist. Living in low-tech times, he engaged people one on one, situation after situation. Living most of his life under the public radar, Jesus demonstrated his vision of mission. He creatively translated his theory of living into deeds of mercy, truth and love. Reflect again on the extent of Jesus' reaching into the darkness of injustice.

Lepers were touched
Women were bestowed with equality
Children were included

Racism was challenged
Second-class citizens were deemed heroes
Drunkards and prostitutes were accepted

Tax collectors changed their behaviour
Pharisees were confronted
Political leaders were resisted

The poor were protected
The rich were humbled
The oppressed were gifted with freedom

Jesus made life right for others. Righteousness was his way of life and he related to others with aspirations for their spiritual well-being. Living his love, Jesus also repeatedly righted wrongs. Jesus' vision for justice for the vulnerable drove his intent and guided his practice. In his teaching and in his living, Jesus created opportunities for people whose plight in life was curtailed by life-denying forces. Jesus envisioned what didn't yet exist. He championed freedom from oppression, exclusion, inequity, sin and injustice.

As followers of Jesus, can we aim to do less?

If Jesus' mission on earth in his time is our mission on earth in our time, we must do more.

As God gives me life and opportunities to serve, I will be listening.

> *Here am I, Lord,*
> *It is I, Lord,*
> *I can hear you calling in the night.*

ENDNOTES

1 McLaren, J. (2004, April 1). Iraq: Looking beyond the hurt. *All the World.*

2 Booth, C. (1859). *Female Ministry: Woman's Right to Preach the Gospel.* Retrieved from http://webapp1.dlib.indiana.edu/vwwp/view?docId=VAB7105.

3 Tuck, T. (2001). Human dignity in an oppressive world. *Word & Deed,* 4 (1), 63-82.

4 *Ibid.*

5 Yamamuro, G. (1922, April). Bushido and The Salvation Army: Some lessons from the Japanese samurai. *The Officer,* 272-276. We are grateful to the account of this story related in Rightmire, R. D. (1997). *Salvationist Samurai: Gunpei Yamamuro and the rise of The Salvation Army in Japan.* Lanham, MD: Scarecrow Press.

6 Booth, W. (1890). *In Darkest England and the Way Out.* Retrieved from http:// www.gutenberg.org/ebooks/475.

7 Clifton, S. (1988). The Salvation Army's action and attitudes in wartime, 1899-1945. *Unpublished PhD dissertation.* University of London.

8 Booth, B. (1977). *Echoes and Memories.* London: Hodder and Stoughton.

9 For more on the ongoing work of the Social Policy and Parliamentary Unit, see http://salvationarmy.org.nz/research-media/social-policy-and-parliamentary-unit/.

10 Millennium Development Goals, http://www.un.org/millenniumgoals/.

11 Universal Declaration of Human Rights, http://www.un.org/en/documents/udhr/.

12   Clifton, S. (2008, October/November). From the General: The address given on the occasion of the official opening of the International Social Justice Commission, New York, August 26, 2008. *The Officer*, 2-4.

13   Gauntlett, S.C. (1933). The Army as a League of Nations. *The Salvation Army Year Book*, 5-6. See also Gauntlett, S. C. (1954). *Social evils the Army has challenged*. London: Hodder and Stoughton.

14   Booth, W. (1890). *In Darkest England and the Way Out.*

15   For more on the match factory, see Coutts, F. (1978). *Bread for my Neighbour: An appreciation of the social action and influence of William Booth*. London: Hodder and Stoughton.

ABOUT THE AUTHORS

An inspiring and effective advocate of justice for all, **M. Christine MacMillan** has been a Salvation Army officer since 1975. In that time, she held leadership appointments in Canada and Bermuda, Australia, Papua New Guinea, England and the United States. In 2007, she became the founding director of The Salvation Army International Social Justice Commission in New York City. Christine's expanding influence includes being chair of the task force on human trafficking for the World Evangelical Alliance and a member of the boards of Health Partners International of Canada and Micah Challenge International.

Don Posterski was part of the global leadership team of World Vision for 17 years. In 2007, he joined the leadership team of The Salvation Army International Social Justice Commission. As a cultural strategist, his consulting practice includes leadership mentoring, research, speaking and writing. Don is the author of several notable books including *True to You: Living out faith in our multi-minded world* (Wood Lake Books, 1995), *Enemies With Smiling Faces* (Intervarsity Press, 2004) and *Elastic Morality* (WestBow Press, 2011).

James E. Read is a senior policy analyst with The Salvation Army International Social Justice Commission and, since 1994, the executive director of The Salvation Army Ethics Centre. He is a professor of philosophy and ethics at Booth University College and speaks and writes on a wide range of issues in social ethics from the perspective of a Christian who has been formed by the convictions of The Salvation Army.